LIFE AND TEACHING OF ŚRĪ ĀNANDAMAYĪ MĀ

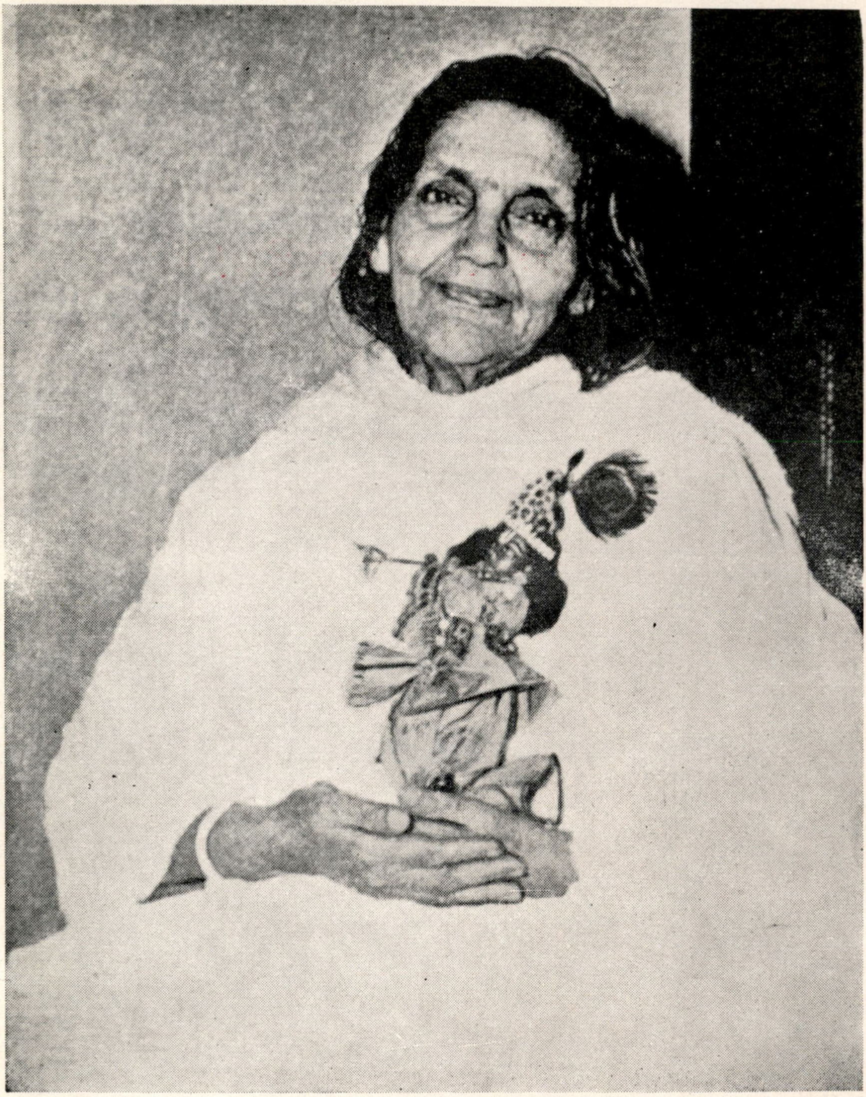

The Mother having Kṛṣṇa's mūrti (idol).

Life And Teaching
Of
Śrī Ānandamayī Mā

DR. ALEXANDER LIPSKI
Director, Religious Studies
Professor of History and Religious Studies,
California State University
Long Beach.

MOTILAL BANARSIDASS
Delhi Varanasi Patna
Bangalore Madras

First Edition: Delhi, 1977
Reprint: Delhi, 1979, 1983, 1988

MOTILAL BANARSIDASS
Bungalow Road, Jawahar Nagar, Delhi 110 007

Branches
Chowk, Varanasi 221 001
Ashok Rajpath, Patna 800 004
24 Race Course Road, Bangalore 560 001
120 Royapettah High Road, Mylapore, Madras 600 004

ISBN: 81-208-0530-5 (Cloth)
ISBN: 81-208-0531-3 (Paper)

PRINTED IN INDIA
BY JAINENDRA PRAKASH JAIN AT SHRI JAINENDRA PRESS, A-45 NARAINA INDUSTRIAL AREA, PHASE I, NEW DELHI 110 028 AND PUBLISHED BY NARENDRA PRAKASH JAIN FOR MOTILAL BANARSIDASS, DELHI 110 007.

TO MY WIFE RUTH-MARIA

PREFACE

"Just imagine that a tree—a beautiful, strong, old beech for instance approaches you with calm steps. What would you feel ? 'Have I gone crazy,' you would ask yourself. 'Or perhaps I am dreaming ?' Finally you would have to concede that you had entered a new dimension of reality of which you had hitherto been ignorant." Thus the German novelist Melita Maschmann sums up her first impressions of Ānandamayī Mā (bliss permeated Mother).

There is no question that Ānandamayī Mā is a spiritual giant who rightfully takes Her place among the great saints of modern India, such as Ramakrishna, Vivekananda, Aurobindo Ghose, Ramana Maharshi and Paramahansa Yogananda. Her life is an eloquent testimony to the abiding strength of Indian spirituality. Her message is particularly appropriate in a world where the notion of progress is no longer taken for gospel truth and the whole array of our "modern values" is undergoing an agonizing reappraisal. Ānandamayī Mā diagnoses the present disease of civilization as "over-secularization". She suggests that the cure from our severe illness cannot be brought about by engineers, sociologists or psychologists but by doctors of the soul. She prescribes a drastic revolution in our views and attitudes from outwardness to inwardness, from materialism to spirituality and from man-centeredness to God-centeredness. Her totally uncompromising transcendent point of view is truly a shock therapy for problem-solving oriented, pragmatic Americans. She shows no apparent concern for the population explosion, environmental pollution, racism, political tensions, economic crises. And yet, as one of Her disciples expressed it, the purpose of Her being is".. to demonstrate the existence of a Power that is ever at work creating by Its transforming influence, Beauty out of ugliness, Love out of strife. Such a Power is Śrī Ānandamayī. May She bring peace and harmony into this world of strife."

I first got interested in Ānandamayī Mā while reading about Her in Paramahansa Yogananda's *Autobiography of a Yogi.*

Subsequently, I met several Americans who had visited Ānandamayī Mā for extended periods of time. In 1965, while spending my sabbatical leave in India, I visited Her ashram in Vārāṇasi and then stayed with Ānandamayī Mā in Rajgir, the capital of an ancient Indian state. When I was brought into the presence of Ānandamayī Mā I felt that, for the first time in my life, I was encountering someone who was the very embodiment of the Holy, the "wholly other." And yet Ānandamayī Mā was also so close and accessible. She immediately welcomed me with a loving smile signifying total acceptance. In Her simple, unaffected way She asked me about my family and with genuine interest looked at the photos of my wife and my three daughters. She then gave me the privilege of sitting near Her. During the ensuing *satsaṅga* I had an opportunity to observe Her at close quarters. I was struck by the youthful almost girlish appearance of the then sixty-nine year old Ānandamayī Mā. It was a delight to listen to Her pearly laughter, and I was struck by the ease and assurance with which the almost illiterate Ānandamayī Mā responded to the most recondite questions of erudite scholars. A highlight of my stay with Ānandamayī Mā was my personal interview during which I was alone with Her except for the presence of an interpreter. Facing Mātājī I felt as though I was mentally stripped naked. It seemed to me that She could see into the innermost recesses of my mind. I asked Her to tell me what the chief obstacles on my spiritual path were. In response She revealed to me some glaring shortcomings of which I had been hitherto totally unaware. What She said was in no way flattering, in fact painful, but Ānandamayī Mā said it so compassionately, although firmly, that I did not feel condemned. I realized what true loving detachment was.

The days at Ānandamayī Mā's Ashram flew by. Throughout my stay I had a feeling of utter contentment and peace—worldly problems were temporarily eclipsed. As though in the presence of a gigantic spiritual magnet my mind was engrossed in the divine. When thinking of the blissful experiences in Rajgir, there flashes even now through my mind a scene of a *kīrtana* with Mātājī. And I hear Her chanting "*He Bhagavān*" (Oh, Lord) to the accompaniment of a harmonium. Her chanting is the very expression of divine love and ecstasy and prompts me to echo the words of the Persian inscription on the Diwan-i-Khās:

If on Earth be an Eden of bliss
It is this, it is this, none but this.

While I had a limited knowledge of Hindi at the time of my visit to Ānandamayī Mā I decided then and there to take up the study of Bengali, to be able to become acquainted in depth with the life and teaching of Mātājī. Through the kind assistance of Mr. K. Bose, Secretary of Shree Shree Ānandamayee Sangha, I was able to procure most of the literature in Bengali and English dealing with Ānandamayī Mā. The more I immersed myself in the life and thought of the bliss permeated Mother, the clearer it became to me that many people in the west could profit from Her wisdom. When I discussed Ānandamayī Mā during my lectures on modern Hindu religious thought I was impressed by the enthusiastic response of the students who eagerly asked for more information about the bliss permeated Mother. This prompted me to undertake the present study. Writing on the life and teaching of Ānandamayī Mā was a privilege in itself, but I am filled with gladness at the thought that through this study Mātājī will become better known and that many spiritual seekers who have become aware of the emptiness of a mere materialistic existence will find renewed meaningfulness.

ALEXANDER LIPSKI

CONTENTS

CHAPTER I

ĀNANDAMAYĪ MĀ'S LĪLĀ

"Before I came on this earth, Father, 'I was the same'. As a little girl, 'I was the same'. I grew into womanhood, but still 'I was the same'....Ever afterwards though the dance of creation changes around me in the hall of eternity, 'I shall be the same'. " These words were addressed by the bliss permeated Mother to Paramahansa Yogananda when he visited Her in Calcutta in 1936. They constitute a challenge to any attempt to superimpose an evolutionary pattern upon Her life. Terms, such as growth, advancement and maturation, as referring to the spiritual aspect of Her life are inapplicable. Yet unquestionably an analysis of Her outward activities shows distinct developmental phases. While according to the Hindu view of life, all manifestation is God's *līlā* (sport, play), the expression seems particularly fitting when dealing with events in the life of Ānandamayī Mā, for She frequently alludes to the fact that She is a detached onlooker, performing voluntarily a play in this delusive earthly theater, on a stage limited by time and space.

Ānandamayī Mā was born on April 30, 1896 in Kheoṛā, a tiny village in the interior of East Bengal (now Bangladesh). British impact was then hardly noticeable in that remote, largely Moslem inhabited area. The house in which She was born was completely surrounded by Moslem dwellings. At that time, fortunately, harmonious relations existed between Moslems and Hindus. Outbreaks of communal violence—chronic occurrences in the twentieth century—were unknown. The majority of the Moslems were converts from low caste Hindus and had still retained traces of their Hindu practices. There were even quite a few devotees of Mother Kālī among the Moslems. Yet it cannot be denied that Hindu caste restrictions constituted an insurmountable barrier preventing a close contact between the two communities.

Ānandamayī Mā's parents were devout Vaiṣṇavas and strict followers of caste regulations. Her father, Bipin Bihārī

Bhaṭṭācārya, came from a distinguished Brāhman family. Most of his time was taken up with religious practices. He especially loved to chant devotional songs. For long periods he would be absent from his home, joining *kīrtana* parties or going on pilgrimages to sacred sites. Her Mother, Mokṣadā Sundarī, counted many pandits among her ancestors. Her family proudly remembered that in the not too distant past one of their ancestors had joyously thrown herself on her dead husband's funeral pyre. Mokṣadā Sundarī shared her husband's fondness for spiritual chants. She even gained some reputation for composing devotional songs which are still popular among the village folk of her region.

Ānandamayī Mā was the second child, born three years after the first—also a daughter—had died at the age of nine months. It is reported that before the birth of Ānandamayī Mā Mokṣadā Sundarī had frequent dreams of gods and goddesses. At birth the future Ānandamayī Mā was given the name Nirmalā Sundarī (Immaculate Beauty). She grew up in an atmosphere of utmost simplicity bordering on penury, since Her father was not much of a provider, the growing family—four brothers and two sisters were born after Nirmalā*—had to live from a small income derived from some minor landed property. Luckily Mokṣadā Sundarī was an exceedingly capable housewife who managed to work veritable miracles with her slender budget. But although Nirmalā never knew starvation, Her education was affected by the family's financial plight. She had to do Her school work on a broken slate because the parents could not afford to buy a new one. At times She could not be "spared" for school, since She had to help with the housework. Then again She missed school because no escort was available and She could not walk there alone. In total, Nirmalā attended school for less than two years. During that short period She impressed the teacher with Her sharp mind. Much later She reminisced: "Somehow or other, I invariably happened to look up the very questions the teacher would ask, and consequently he always found me well prepared even after long absences. The meaning of unknown words would occur to me spontaneously..." With less than two years of Primary School to

* Only one brother, Makhan, is still alive at the time of writing.

Her credit, Ānandamayī Mā can hardly be considered "educated" Although She is capable of writing* She normally autographs books with a mere dot. When doing so, She sometimes remarks: "In this everything is contained". She never sees fit to read books, and thus just like the equally "uneducated" Ramakrishna Paramahansa, testifies to the fact that wisdom is not dependent on book learning—a truth too shocking to be accepted by most academicians. The bliss permeated Mother Herself once stated: "If someone really wants God, and nothing but God, he carries his book in his own heart. He needs no printed book."

From early childhood on Nirmalā exhibited a cheerful disposition, so that Her neighbours nicknamed Her *Hāsi Mā* (Mother of Smiles) or *Khusīr Mā* (Happy Mother). She felt equally at home among Hindus and Moslems. Her orthodox mother, naturally, insisted on safeguarding Nirmalā from contamination. Ritual purity had to be preserved: "As long as *annaprāśana* (ceremony when a baby first takes solid food at about five or six months) has not taken place, it is no sin to touch a Moslem. After that such contact requires an ablution." Many an ablution had to be administered to the Mother of Smiles ! She also met the first Christians while still a child. When Christian missionaries came to Kheoṛā and pitched a tent there, Nirmalā visited them and was greatly impressed by their sincerity and devoutness. She loved to listen to their hymn singing and begged Her mother to buy Her one of their Bengali hymn books. Many years later, in 1962, some German visitors sang Christian hymns to Ānandamayī Mā. She thoroughly enjoyed them and mentioned to the Germans that hearing the hymns reminded Her of Her childhood experience in Kheoṛā.

Nirmalā had no formal religious education. Normally in India children absorb religion by osmosis. They observe the adults and as soon as is feasible participate in *pūjā* (worship). Thus the little Nirmalā learnt devotional chanting from Her

* There is one specimen of Her writing (probably from 1930). She wrote: "O thou Supreme Being, thou art manifest in all forms—this universe, with all created things, wife, husband, father, mother and children, all in one. Man's mind is clouded by worldly ties. But there is no cause for despair. With purity, unflinching faith and burning eagerness go ahead and you will realize your true Self." (Trans. from Bengali)

father and was soon seen joining him eagerly in daily worship. There were some early signs that the little Mother of Smiles was not an ordinary child, but the parents did not grasp their import. One day, for example, She casually asked Her mother: "Ma, did not Mr. Nandan Cakravartī visit us shortly after I was born ?" The mother was taken aback. It was true that a Mr. Cakravartī had called on them when Nirmalā was just a few days old, but they had never referred to his visit. How could Nirmalā possibly remember it ? There were a few other instances suggesting that She must have been fully conscious of Her surroundings practically from the time of birth on. Also, once in a while She had spells of absentmindedness—obviously trances. Then again She was seen talking to plants and to apparently invisible beings. These instances were, however, rare, so that the parents were not unduly alarmed. Her cheerfulness and lovability more than compensated for Her occasional strange behaviour. Her obedience was truly remarkable. Once a relative left Her in front of the local Śiva temple and told Her to remain there until her return. The relative became so involved in some errand that she forgot about Nirmalā. Many hours later, when she returned to the temple, she found the little girl sitting in the very position in which she had left Her.

One incident of Her early childhood reveals the fact that the smiling and submissive Nirmalā was capable of a fiery disposition and that She could wield superhuman power. Apparently Her grandmother felt that Nirmalā liked to eat more than Her fair share of the scanty supply of food that was available. One day, when Nirmalā was about four or five years old, She brought to Her grandmother a pot filled to the brim with curds. Her grandmother was greatly irritated believing that Nirmalā had filled the pot to overflow, expecting to receive an extra large helping. The grandmother scolded Nirmalā severely and told Her she would receive no curds at all that day. At that instant the pot cracked and all the curds leaked out. The grandmother never again withheld curds from her uncanny grand-daughter.

As was customary at that time, a husband had to be found for the Mother of Smiles while She was still a child. The prospective husband had to be of the proper caste, i.e., a Brāhman and his family had to accept the fact that the dowry would be minimal.

After a careful search the parents arranged for the marriage of Nirmalā to Ramaṇi Mohan Cakravartī, later referred to as Bholānātha (a name for Śiva). He was the third son of Jagatbandhu Cakravartī and Tripura Sundari Devi who lived in Aṭpāṛā, a village in the district of Dacca. The marriage took place on February 7th, 1909, when Nirmalā was not quite thirteen years of age. While the age of Bholānāth is nowhere mentioned, it is known that he was considerably older than his wife. For the next five years the couple did not live together. Bholānāth, who had a very rudimentary education, was a clerk in the police department at Aṭpāṛā at the time of marriage. After a few months he lost that job and for the next few years moved around all over East Bengal, finding temporary employment only. Until 1910 Nirmalā continued to live with Her parents. When She was fourteen years of age it seemed appropriate to send Her to Her husband's family, there to be prepared for Her future household duties. Ordinarily Her mother-in-law would have been in charge of Her. But, since Bholānāth's mother had died two years before his marriage, the function of training his wife devolved upon Pramodā Devī, the wife of his eldest brother, Revatī Mohan. This was in accordance with the hierarchical family order of India. In 1910, therefore, Nirmalā moved to Śrīpur, where Revatī Mohan's family lived. Revatī Mohan was employed as a station-master on the Dacca-Jagannathgunj line. Both Revatī Mohan and Pramodā Devī became exceedingly fond of the little Mother of Smiles who adapted Herself easily to Her new environment, charming everyone with Her joyfulness. She took over practically all the household chores and soon excelled in spinning, needlework, weaving, and especially in cooking. She worked so hard at scrubbing pots and keeping the house clean that Her hands were covered with bruises. Many years later, when Her fame had already spread all over India, She met with Her sister-in-law, and the two exchanged happy reminiscences about village life in Śrīpur. Ānandamayī Mā acted completely naturally, as though She was still the young village girl. In front of a crowd of devotees, She said teasingly: "Look, all these housewives think that they are great experts in household work. Tell them whether I too did not look after your house satisfactorily ?" Pramodā Devī eagerly assented to this. Indeed she had had reason to be greatly satisfied with her highly efficient and utterly obedient sister-in-law. The four years in Śrīpur were, at least outwardly, rather uneventful as far as Nirmalā's spiritual līlā is concerned. There were just a few instances of trances. Several times Pramodā Devī was attracted by the smell of burnt food to the kitchen, where she found Nirmalā unconscious on the kitchen floor. But Pramodā Devī was unsuspecting. She assumed that her hard working sister-in-law had fallen asleep from fatigue. Nirmalā's life in Śrīpur came to an end in 1913, a few months after Her brother-in-law Revatī Mohan had died. For about six months She stayed with Her parents. Then, in 1914, She joined Bholānāth in Aṣṭagrāma, also in East Bengal, where he had found employment in the Land Settlement Department. This was the actual beginning of their life together.

A most unusual marriage it was to be. So far Bholānāth had had no inkling of Nirmalā's extraordinary state. He had thought that he had married an ordinary village girl. He was slightly disappointed that She proved even less educated than he. At first he had sent Her books hoping to interest Her in improving Her reading but soon he realized that his wife had no scholarly inclinations. When he first tried to approach Her physically, he supposedly received such a violent electric shock that he put for the time being all thought of a physical relationship out of his mind. He seems to have initially thought that this was only a temporary condition, that Nirmalā was still such a child and that She would later become "normal". But the marriage was never physically consummated. As far as Nirmalā is concerned, the question of sexual desire did not even arise. In 1938, after Bholānāth's death, She told Didi:* "There never was any shadow of a worldly thought in Bholānāth's mind. He made no difference between me and little Maroṇi (his sister's grand-daughter) when we lay near him at night. You will remember that many times when you were going away at night, you laid me down near him when this body** was in a *bhāva* (ecstasy). He was never troubled by any self-consciousness. In Bajītpur, as well as in Shah-bagh, he guarded and looked

* Didi, Gurupriyā Devi, one of Her closest devotees. See p. 18.

** Ānandamayī Mā refers to Herself usually as "this body" or as "this little daughter of yours." She usually addresses all unmarried people as Her friends and married people as Her fathers or mothers.

after this body most confidently and unselfconsciously. Once or twice, when there was an inkling of a worldly thought in him which was so unformed as not to be on the level of his consciousness, this body would assume all the symptoms of death. He would feel frightened and do *japa* (repetition of a mantra or a name of God) knowing that he could re-establish contact with me by that method alone."

It is quite obvious that Bholānāth showed an exceptional degree of self-control. It may also be assumed that Nirmalā helped him to live a celibate life by virtue of Her own spiritual power and not just through "shock treatment." Bholānāth himself must have been an unusual person, considering the fact that he was willing to accept this most unconventional marriage. One must bear in mind that his position was particularly anomalous for India, where traditionally women were looked upon as inferior to men. A wife was expected to be submissive to her husband and to worship him as a god. The *Rāmāyaṇa* aptly compares the relation of a wife to her husband to that of a shadow to the substance. Actually Nirmalā's relation to Bholānāth was complex. On the one hand, She was spiritually his superior and later became his guru. On the other hand, She played the role of an obedient wife. Her mother had enjoined upon Her: "Now you must look upon your husband as your guardian and obey and respect him, just as you did your own parents." Initially She obeyed him in all matters and carried out Her household duties promptly and efficiently. But when Her *kheyāla** inspired Her to act in a certain way, She would brook no opposition. Formally She would always ask his approval before any undertaking, but if his approval was not forthcoming, She would find means to bring about his assent. As Her spiritual status became known and Her life style underwent changes, new problems arose, further challenging the traditional husband-wife relationship. Whenever Ānandamayī Mā decided to travel without Bholānāth, She not only needed his permission to do so but She was required to travel in the company of some respectable elder male, preferably a relative, to preserve "propriety". Also, as people found out about Her exalted

* Normally sudden desire; in Ānandamayi Mā's case, a spontaneous manifestation of divine will. See p. 33.

spiritual state, they started to come for *darśana* (literally sight, vision; being blessed by the presence of a saint). This conflicted with the prevailing *purdāh* rules, according to which a young married woman had to be heavily veiled and would normally not be in sight of men. Bholānāth proved uncommonly generous in that respect. Under the circumstances he exposed himself to severe criticism from friends and relatives alike. When Nirmalā's spiritual "eccentricities" became more apparent, his relatives urged him to separate from Her and to find a "regular" wife who could provide him with sons, the normal aspiration of every householder. He staunchly resisted these suggestions, even though this was hard for him, given the fact that he was so fond of his family and that there is evidence that he would have liked to have a normal home life. One can only conjecture about his inner conflicts, since he left no memoirs behind. It will, however, become clear from the subsequent events that Ānandamayī Mā subtly moulded Her husband-disciple until he was able successfully to cope with all of life's problems. Eventually he must have felt that he was amply compensated for the lack of a conventional family life by reaping a rich spiritual harvest.

How did Ānandamayī Mā regard Her husband? When he once asked Her, in the presence of many of Her devotees, whether She did not love him a little more than others, She retorted emphatically that this was not so. But we do have a statement from Her expressing Her appreciation of Bholānāth: "All of you know that Bholānāth was prone to fits of great anger. It is said that even *Ṛṣis* (saints, seers) were subject to the emotion of anger. Not that I am saying that Bholānāth was a *Ṛṣi*. If I did, people would think I was praising my husband. But you have all seen for yourselves that he led an extraordinary life of self-denial and rigorous asceticism."

That Bholānāth was married to a spiritually exalted woman was first recognized during their stay in Astagrāma. Bholānāth and Nirmalā lived in the house of one Sārada Sankar Sen. It was Sen's brother-in-law, Hara Kumār Ray, who "discovered" Her superior spirituality. A well-educated but emotionally unstable person, Hara Kumār Ray was often overtaken by extreme religious fervour and then was unable to attend to his work, some kind of clerical job. Shortly before Nirmalā's arrival in Astagrāma he had lost his mother. It so happened that Nirmalā and Bholānāth occupied the very room where his mother had been living. When he first met Nirmalā he spontaneously prostrated himself in front of Her and addressed Her as "Mā" (mother). From then on he seized every opportunity to be of service to Her. Soon he pleaded with Bholānāth to be permitted to see Mā daily, to talk to Her and to receive from Her *prasāda* (food offered to a deity or a saint becomes *prasāda*, when it has been accepted by the deity, and it is subsequently distributed to worshippers). Bholānāth agreed and even told Nirmalā who had so far not reacted to Hara Kumār Ray's pleading, to talk to him and to give him *prasāda*. One day while paying his worshipful respects to Nirmalā, Hara Kumār exclaimed: "..(now) I am calling you "Mā", one day the whole world will call you so," a prophetic statement. Hara Kumār Ray vanished from Mā's life as suddenly as he had appeared. Later on She received a few letters from him in which he addressed Her as *devi* (goddess). Hara Kumār was not the only person in Astagrāma who sensed that Nirmalā was not just an ordinary human being. One of Bholānāth's friends, Kṣetra Mohan, also prostrated himself before Her and addressed Her as "Goddess Durgā." Further attention was drawn to the Mother when She entered a trance during a *kīrtana*. So far Her trances had occurred in the privacy of their home. In this instance it was observed by many of the villagers.

In 1916 Mā became seriously ill and was moved to Vidyakut near Kheoṛā where Her parents were living at that time. During Her stay in Vidyakut Mā showed that She was able to discriminate between genuine spiritual attainment and mere posing. One of Her cousins, Annapūrṇa, had spells of trance-like states, and the gullible village folk started worshipping her. When Mā encountered Annapūrṇa in a "trance," She immediately knew that Annapūrṇa was far from having an ecstatic experience, but that the trancelike state was brought about by her grief over the absence of her husband. She "cured" Her cousin by whispering into her ear that Annapūrṇa would soon receive a letter from her beloved. In later years the Mother "cured" other seeming saints, and She strongly warned against false sādhus and spiritual fraud in general.

Mā remained with Her parents in Vidyakut until 1918 when

She joined Bholānāth in Bajītpur. He had found employment on one of the estates of the *Nawab** of Dacca. The next six years (1918-1924), the Bajītpur phase, is usually referred to as the "play of *sādhanā*".[1] Concerning Her *sādhanā*, She explained in retrospect to one of Her devotees: "Let me tell you that what I am, I have been from my infancy. But when the different stages of *sādhanā* were being manifested through this body there was something like superimposition of *ajñāna* (ignorance). But what sort of *ajñāna* was that ? It was really *jñāna* (knowledge) masquerading as *ajñāna*..." She further elaborated on the unusual nature of Her *sādhanā*: "One day in Bajītpur I went to bathe in a pond near the house where we lived. While I was pouring water over my body, the *kheyāla* suddenly came to me, 'How would it be to play the role of a *sādhikā* (one who practises *sādhanā*)'. And so the *līlā* began."

The question why Self-realized masters practise *sādhanā* has been debated in Indian relgious literature. In the case of Ramakirshna his devotees maintain that he engaged in *sādhanā* voluntarily as an inspiration to his disciples. From the available account of his life it appears that he had to make a determined effort to gain union with the One. In particular he struggled to free himself from the concept of God in the form of Mother Kālī to reach the formless *Brahman* (absolute). Moreover he had the guidance of various gurus throughout his *sādhanā*. Very different is the case of the Mother. There is no evidence of striving to attain anything. She never had a guru. Also, She was totally unacquainted with religious scriptures. We thus witness the spontaneous unfoldment of a *līlā*, rather than a *sādhanā*. At night the Mother would be seen sitting in a corner of their room uttering various mantras and assuming countless complicated *āsanas* (postures). She comments: "When the different stages of *sādhanā* were being manifested through this body, what a variety of experiences I then had ! Sometimes I used to hear distinctly: 'Repeat this mantra.' When I got the mantra a query arose in me: 'Whose mantra is this ?' At once the reply came: 'It is the mantra of Gaṇesh (elephant headed god, son of Śiva) or of Viṣṇu,' or something like that. Again

* *Nawab* Deputy; a Moslem administrative title.

1. *Sādhanā* spiritual discipline for the purpose of attaining Self-realization.

the query came from myself: 'How does he look ?' A form was revealed in no time. Every question was met by a prompt reply and there was immediate dissolution of all doubts and misgivings. One day I distinctly got the command: 'From today you are not to bow down to anybody.' I asked my invisible monitor: 'Who are you ?' The reply came: 'Your *Śakti* (power).' I thought that there was a distinct *Śakti* residing in me and guiding me by issuing commands from time to time. Since all this happened at the stage of *sādhanā*, *jñāna* was being revealed in a piece-meal fashion. The integral knowledge which this body was possessed of from the very beginning was broken, as it were, into parts and there was something like the superimposition of ignorance... After some time I again heard the voice within myself which told me: 'Whom do you want to make obedience to ? You are everything.' At once I realized that the Universe was all my own manifestation. Partial knowledge then gave place to the integral, and I found myself face to face with the One that appears as many. It was then that I understood why I had been forbidden for so long to bow to anybody." During that period various *vibhuti* (supernormal powers) manifested. She cured people from all sorts of diseases by merely touching them.

The nightly spectacle of Mā's *sādhanā* filled Bholānāth with extreme awe. The ecstatically blissful Mā chanted often for hours, repeating the name of Hari (name for Viṣṇu). This displeased Bholānāth who was not a Vaiṣṇava like his wife, but a *Śākta* (worshipper of Śiva's consort, Kālī or Durgā). He therefore urged Mā to chant the name of Śiva or Kālī. She instantly complied with his request, fully cognizant of the fact that all divine names are equally effective.

In the beginning Mā engaged in *sādhanā* only at night when no one but Bholānāth could observe Her. Soon, however, mantras and Sanskrit stanzas flowed from Her lips in the presence of outsiders. Witnessing Her unconventional behaviour, the neighbours became suspicious and some even concluded that the Mother of Smiles was possessed by evil spirits. No longer did She enjoy unqualified popularity. Bholānāth was placed in an awkward position, experiencing the pressure of friends and neighbours to put an end to the improper behaviour of his wife. He felt compelled to summon several *ojhās* (spirit exorcisers) to "cure" his wife. One *ojhā* received a drastic lesson while trying to free Mā from evil spirits. When he touched Her he was seized with such a pain that he fell writhing to the ground. Upon Bholānāth's pleading, Mā removed the pain, whereupon the *ojhā* prostrated himself in front of Her and then left in a hurry. Eventually Bholānāth consulted a distinguished physician, Dr. Mahendra C. Nandi. After observing Mā, he assured Bholānāth that She did not suffer from mental illness but showed obvious signs of being God-intoxicated. This reminds one of Ramakrishna who too was for a time suspected of mental imbalance while actually experiencing divine ecstasy. Even in spiritual India, worldliness is the normal state of mankind, and extreme God-centeredness is so rare that it is understandably considered madness. A comparison of Mā's *sādhanā* with that of Ramakrishna shows that both went rapidly through spiritual disciplines which normally require a life time of practice, and both followed various Hindu as well as non-Hindu religious practices. In the case of Mā, however, except for a few vague statements, no details regarding the performance of non-Hindu rites are available. It was the night of *jhūlan pūrṇimā**. She had prepared Her husband's evening meal and had just started Her customary nocturnal worship, when She received the inspiration to enact the role of a guru and of a *śiṣya* (disciple) simultaneously. The *bīja mantra* (seed mantra; mantra of initiation) proceeded from Her lips spontaneously and She repeated it with the realization that guru, *śiṣya* and mantra were one. Mā explained the underlying meaning of initiation: "God Himself in the role of the spiritual preceptor (Guru) discloses His name to the pilgrim wandering in search of a guide." There is no other known instance of self-initiation. This lends further weight to the view that in the person of Mā we are faced with a unique phenomenon.

During the months following Mā's initiation, Her *sādhanā* grew in intensity. She tells us that She had visions of various deities of the Hindu pantheon. Bholānāth often observed that She identified Herself with a particular deity and subsequently worshipped that very deity. Underlying all Her worship was

* Full moon swing festival in August. At that time images of Rādhā and Kṛṣṇa are placed in swings.

the theme of Oneness: Worshipper, worshipping and the object of Her worship merged. During that phase She was hardly conscious of Her body and only occasionally touched food or felt the need to sleep.

Naturally there was concern and even indignation among some of Her relatives when Her unconventional behaviour continued. One of Her cousins in particular was shocked that She had initiated Herself while Her husband had not yet been initiated. The head of the household was thus placed in a position spiritually inferior to his wife. When the cousin challenged Mā, She assured him that Bholānāth would receive initiation in five months' time. Early in December 1922, She Herself initiated Her husband—another break with spiritual convention. In this connection it should be stressed that She carried out the initiation ceremony in accordance with the rules laid down in the *śāstras* (scriptures), even though She was not acquainted with them.

Following Bholānāth's initiation, for a period of three years, Mā remained in complete silence, which She only rarely interrupted for the purpose of either comforting someone in deep distress or to convey an important message. While She was still in silence, Bholānāth lost his position in Bajītpur and decided to move to Dacca, the chief city in East Bengal, in April, 1924. In Dacca the chances of finding permanent employment seemed more favourable than in the villages or small towns where they had lived up to that time. On April 17th, 1924, Bholānāth secured work with his former employer, the Nawab of Dacca. He was appointed Manager of the Nawab's extensive estate, the Shah-bagh gardens. There in a small house Mā's *līlā* continued. It so happened that several acquaintances from Bajītpur had also moved to Dacca. Through them the news about Mā's exalted status spread rapidly, attracting the first real devotees to the "Mother of Shah-bagh gardens." Among them were Prāṇ Gopāl Mukherji, Deputy Postmaster General of Dacca and family, Nishikanta Mitra, a *zamindār* (landowner) and family, Nani Gopāl Banerji, a professor at Dacca College, Baul Chandra Basak, lecturer at Vakil Institute. It is significant that all of the devotees were *bhadraloks* (respectable people, gentlemen, a privileged minority from the highest castes, usually landed or professionals, always well educated) who came to sit at the feet of the practically illiterate Mā. One is reminded of another *bhadralok*, Pratap Candra Mazumdar, who explained why he, a westernized intellectual, sat at the feet of the illiterate Ramakrishna: "His religion is ecstasy, his worship means transcendental insight..." Similarly, being in the presence of the "Mother of Shah-bagh gardens" seemed transcendental bliss to Her followers.

We are fortunate to have an account by a Dr. Nalini Kanta Brahma of his visit to Shah-bagh, which enables us to recapture at least to some extent the atmosphere prevailing there. "It was a cold evening in December 1924, when I was taken to Shah-bagh for a *darśana* of the Mother by Rai Bahadur Prāṇ Gopāl Mukherji, the then Deputy Postmaster General of Dacca. He had already secured the permission of Her husband for the purpose and we were taken straight to the room where Mother was sitting alone deeply absorbed in meditation. A dim lamp was burning in front of Her and that was perhaps the only thing in the room. Mother's face was completely hidden from our view as in those days She used to veil it exactly like a newly married village girl...After we had waited there for about half an hour, suddenly the veil loosened itself and Mother's face became visible in all its brilliance and lustre. Hymns containing many seed mantras began to be recited by the Mother in uncommon accents, producing wonderful resonance, which affected the whole surroundings. The stillness of the cold December night, the loneliness of the Shah-bagh gardens and above all the sublimity and serenity of the atmosphere in the Mother's room—all combined to produce a sense of holiness. As long as we were in the room, we felt an indescribable elevation of the spirit, a silence and a depth not previously experienced, a peace that passeth all understanding..."

While in Shah-bagh, Mā was seen to be more frequently than ever in trancelike states. On several occasions Her husband found Her unconscious, on the point of drowning in the pond near their house into which She had fallen while cleaning the kitchen ware. Bholānāth concluded that he could not leave Her all by Herself at home. He asked his widowed sister, Mātarī, whom Mā had befriended while living in his eldest brother's home, to stay with them and look after his wife. Mā became increasingly friendly with Mātarī. Their close relation-

The Mother of Shah-bagh Gardens.

ship lasted until Mātarī's death in 1959. Meanwhile, in August 1924, Mā's younger sister Surabalā had died at the age of sixteen. Assuming that Mā must be deeply grieved by the death of Her sister, Bholānāth arranged for Her parents to join the household in Shah-bagh. It was his hope that the presence of Her parents would help Mā bear the loss of Her sister. Little did he as yet understand Nirmalā for whom death held no dread. Conscious of the oneness of all existence, Mā was totally unaffected by the *līlā* of life and death: "Come what may, what does it matter?"

Mā's first year in Shah-bagh is also memorable for the discovery of Siddheśvarī. During Her stay in Bajītpur She had had a vision of a sacred site in the neighbourhood of Dacca by the name of Siddheśvarī. Upon inquiry in Dacca She was finally led to an abandoned, almost inaccessible Kālī temple in the midst of a wilderness. Further investigation revealed that Siddheśvarī had numerous associations with great saints and sages of the past. Śaṅkarācārya, the greatest exponent of *advaita* (monism) (788-820 A.D.) is supposed to have spent some time there. From September 1924 on, Mā frequently stayed overnight in the Kālī temple of Siddheśvarī. In 1928 an āśram was built at Siddheśvarī, the first of a network of āśrams all over northern India, to be nuclei for worship and the spreading of Mā's teaching.

Meanwhile the little house in Shah-bagh became a veritable magnet for *darśana* seekers. Bholānāth intuitively knew that he must disregard conventions and set aside all feelings of possessiveness to make Mā accessible to the public. When Her silence ended in October 1925, he let the devotees talk freely with Her. Bholānāth ignored Mā's warning: "You must think twice before you open the doors to the world in this manner. Remember that you will not be able to stem the tide when it becomes overwhelming." And the tide was approaching, threatening to engulf what little privacy the young couple had enjoyed.

Mā's first public appearance occurred in connection with Kālī *pūjā*, the festival in honour of the Divine Mother in Her terrifying aspect which is confined to Bengal. Reluctantly She had agreed to conduct the Kālī *pūjā* in 1925. During the ceremony She deviated from common practice by placing flowers and sandal paste upon Her own head instead of the idol, obviously implying that She was the true reflection of Kālī and not the image. It is reported that: "All that time Mother's face glowed with an intense uncommon beauty and throughout the ceremony there was a spell of great sanctity and deep absorption over all the people present." She did permit the sacrifice of a goat as was customary on this occasion, but She saw to it that in subsequent Kālī *pūjā* celebrations in which She participated no animal was sacrificed. The true meaning of animal sacrifice, She explained, was sacrificing one's lower (animal) nature, living up to the fact that it was man's destiny to raise himself to his inherent divine status.

Mā's *līlā* assumed constantly new features, mystifying, thrilling, often overwhelming Her devotees. On January 26, 1926, a *kīrtana* was performed at Shah-bagh on the occasion of the solar eclipse. We have a most vivid description of the happenings at the *kīrtana:* "At one moment Mātājī (mother) was sitting like one of us. The next moment She had changed completely. Her body started swaying rhythmically...With Her body still swaying, She stood up or rather was drawn upwards on Her toes. It looked as if Mātājī had left Her body which had become an instrument in the hands of an invisible power...She circled round the room as if wafted along by the wind. Occasionally, Her body would start falling to the ground—but before it completed the movement it would regain its upright position, just like a wind-blown leaf which flutters towards the ground and then is uplifted and blown forward by a fresh gust of wind. It seemed Her body had no weight or substance...Before the crowd had time to realize that She was in their midst, She fell to the ground from an upright position but did not appear to be hurt at all. Like a leaf in a whirlwind, Her body started rolling at tremendous speed while She was lying prostrate...After a few moments, Her body of its own accord, stopped moving and Mātājī sat up. Now She was still like a statue...Her face was flushed and radiant and there was an effulgence all around Her." After a while She sang with a heavenly voice:

O Hari, O Murāri, O foe of Kaiṭabha and Madhu.
*O Gopāl, O Govinda, O Mukunda, O Śauri !**

At Mā's suggestion nightly *kīrtanas* were instituted at Shahbagh. At those *kīrtanas* She exhibited varying aspects of rapture.

* Kaiṭabha and Madhu were two demons killed by Viṣṇu. All other names are various epithets of Viṣṇu or Kṛṣṇa.

Watching the nocturnal miraculous events, the devotees became convinced that Her body was possessed by divine forces for the purpose of manifesting the infinite beauty of the cosmic creation. Not only *kīrtanas* but specific events in nature, such as the sight of rippling waves, brought about ecstatic states in the Mother. Here again one can find a similarity in the life of Ramakrishna who experienced ecstasy at the sight of a thundercloud.

In October, 1926, Mā was again asked to perform Kālī *pūjā*. Once more She deviated from the normal ritual. When the *pūjā* was drawing to a close and *pūrṇāhuti* (the final burnt offering of a sacrifice) arrived, She did not permit it to be offered. Instead She suggested that the sacrificial fire be preserved—it is still kept burning at Her āśrams in Vārāṇasi where it was transferred at the time of the Partition in 1947* and in Dehradun and Naimishāraṇya. As a rule, at the conclusion of a *pūjā*, the image is immersed in the holy Ganges. At the request of a devotee, the Mother, however, gave instructions to keep the idol. It was later placed in Her āśram at Ramna (near the race course in Dacca) and on Her birthday it was made accessible for *darśana* to people of all castes and creeds. Mā thus made a liberalizing innovation approximately ten years ahead of Mahatma Gandhi's campaign for opening temples to all castes.

The regular performance of Hindu rites on the Nawab's property did not encounter opposition from the Moslems. In fact Mā gained the respect and affection of the Nawab's family and of Moslems in general. The Moslem community had good reasons to be fond of the Mother of Shah-bagh gardens, as She frequently gave indications of Her reverence for Islam. In Shah-bagh there happened to be the grave of a Moslem faqur. Once Ānandamayī Mā was seen performing *namāz* (Moslem prayer) at his grave. Spontaneously a prayer issued from Her lips which was identified by some bystanders as Arabic verses from the Koran. During a *kīrtana*, Ānandamayī Mā noticed a Moslem watching Her from a distance. She moved towards him with a welcoming gesture, chanting: "Allah, Allahu Akbar (God is great)." On another occasion She walked up to some Moslem workmen and got them to chant in unison the praises

* The same fire was used for the great sacrifice from 1947-1950. See also page 58.

of Allah. Gradually She acquired a number of devoted Moslem disciples. Even after the Partition, when Mā could no longer visit Her homeland, East Bengal, She retained a core of loyal Moslem followers there. They looked after Her āśrams and provided the necessary financial means for their upkeep. As far as Mā is concerned, Hindus and Moslems or adherents of other religions ultimately are one: "*Kīrtana* and *Namāz* are one and the same."

While Mā was attracting Moslems, the majority of Her followers are Hindus. In 1925-26 some of Her greatest devotees who constituted the inner circle of Her ever expanding spiritual family were drawn to Her. In the beginning of 1926, Dr. Sasanka Mohan Mukhopadhyaya, a retired Civil Surgeon and his second eldest daughter Adarini Devī (now known as Gurupriyā Devī or Didi, i.e. elder sister) came to Her. Dr. Mukhopadhyaya, who had been used to worldly comforts, eventually became a renunciant under the Mother's purifying influence. Didi, a deeply religious girl, had thwarted Her parents' earlier plans to have Her married. She immediately attracted Mā's attention: "Where have you been all this time ?" This reminds one of Ramakrishna's similar exclamation upon meeting Narendranath Datta, the future Swami Vivekananda. Didi became Mā's close assistant and helped Her first with household duties and later with the administration of the various āśrams. It is to her that we owe the most extensive record of Ānandamayī Mā's *līlā*—a total of seventeen volumes in Bengali and nineteen in Hindi chronicling the daily events in Her life have been published so far. If Didi can be considered Her most intimate woman devotee, Her most advanced man devotee was Jyotiścandra Ray, later known as Bhāijī (brother), Personal Assistant to the Director of Agriculture of Bengal. Bhāijī met Her towards the end of 1924. Shortly afterwards Ānandamayī Mā told him: "There is a very subtle close spiritual link between this body and yourself." Towards the end of his life Bhāijī wrote what is probably the most insightful account of his experiences with Mā, entitled *Mother as Revealed to me*. In it he relates the genesis of the name Ānandamayī Mā. One afternoon, while he was busy at work, the Mother summoned him to Shah-bagh. Upon his arrival there She informed him that he was to accompany Her and Bholānāth to Siddheśvarī. While She was sitting near the Kālī temple at Siddheśvarī it occurred to him all of a sudden to suggest to Bholānāth: "From today we shall call Mother by the name of Ānandamayī." Bholānāth instantly agreed. The following day, when he asked the Mother why She had ordered him to interrupt his office duties, She responded laughingly: "If you had not come, who else would have given a name to this body." A remark such as this leads one to conclude that the bliss permeated Mother is perfectly attuned to the cosmic *līlā*—everything unfolds at the proper time and under the proper circumstances. Hamlet-like doubt is alien to Her. She often says: "Whatever is to be, will be."

Around this time (1926), people started coming regularly to Ānandamayī Mā, expecting Her to cure them from physical ailments. She made it clear to Her devotees that She could not indiscriminately effect cures, but only when She was "prompted" to do so. There were times when She had distinct indications that She was not to heal. In such cases She simply informed the person in question that it was not his destiny to be cured by Her. Discussing the subject of healing and other so-called supernatural powers, She explained that such powers often come to spiritual seekers as a byproduct of their *sādhanā*. But powers per se must never become the goal. One should accept such manifestations humbly and with equanimity, always keeping in mind that God-realization is the only worthwhile objective.

Ānandamayī Mā continued to be a constant reminder of the fact that unlimited powers can be manifested through the instrumentality of the human body. Already in Bajītpur, She had surprised Her devotees by eating unusually small amounts of food. Some time in 1924, She lost Her ability to feed Herself. Her fingers simply refused to hold on to food. No "satisfactory" explanation is available to account for the loss of what normally is considered a vital function. Yet it appears that Her "handicap" may perhaps be meant to demonstrate that eating is less of a basic need than man ordinarily thinks. From that time on, the bliss permeated Mother has been fed by others, first by Bholānāth and then chiefly by Didi. Recently, other younger devotees have taken over this duty. Feeding Ānandamayī Mā has been problematic. Initially She accepted absurdly small quantities of food or refused to eat altogether. Once She abstained from all food and drink for twenty-three days. This is most unusual, considering that the great Gandhi took in at least some liquid while fasting. For half a year Ānandamayī Mā lived on a daily diet of six grains of boiled rice and two or three ripe fruits which—She insisted—must have fallen from trees. If no fruit had fallen off in a natural way, She would forgo eating fruit on that day. The disconcerting thing about Ānandamayī Mā was that well-meaning devotees found out that it was impossible to deceive Her and pretend that a fruit had fallen off a tree. Once, after She had not touched any food for days, Bholānāth expressed his concern for Her well-being. The next day She ate all the *purees* (fried unleavened brown bread) that were available, completely exhausting the household supply of flour and ghee (clarified butter). And She warned: "Had there been more I would have eaten them all. I tell you, do not make arrangements for me. If I really start eating none of you will be able to provide for me, however rich you may be." In fact, once She ate forty pounds of pudding meant for a large party. Yet She suffered none of the consequences attendant upon gluttony. The bliss permeated Mother is a concrete example of what Heinrich Zimmer* calls "The phenomenon of expanding form." Just as in Hindu mythology the pigmy Vāman manages with one step to reach beyond the sun, so too Ānandamayī Mā can, if She desires, eat superhuman quantities of food. Essentially She tries to teach by example that humanity is far too food-conscious, and that most people grossly overeat. The body requires only a small amount of food. The remainder, eaten out of habit, because it is pleasurable, is wasted. Through yoga, She avers, man can free himself from dependence upon food and imbibe by spiritual means the necessary energy from his surroundings. Being conscious of the Oneness underlying the multiple manifestation, She is able to extract whatever She "needs" out of "air". Thus She is a living example of Christ's saying that "Man does not live by bread alone." Hoarding of food draws Her special censure. Noticing an undue amount of stocked food in the home of a Calcutta devotee, She went to his storage room and had all the food distributed among the neighbourhood families.

* Heinrich Zimmer, *Myths and Symbols in Indian Art and Civilization*, Harper Torchbooks, 1962.

Ānandamayī Mā could not only transcend the need for food whenever She so desired, but, according to Bhāijī, She could often be seen in the breathless state of *samādhi.* He describes one of those instances: "Her face glowed with a crimson hue due to the intensity of inner *ānandam* (bliss): Her cheeks shone with a heavenly light, Her forehead looked bright and serene with a divine calm. All Her physical expressions were suspended; yet from every pore of Her body radiated an uncommon glow—a mute eloquence of silent, inner speech. Everybody present felt that Mother was sinking into the depths of divine communion. Thus passed some ten to twelve hours..." Bhāijī was also fortunate to be present when Ānandamayī Mā revealed that She had had a direct experience of man's spiritual anatomy. She had clearly seen the working of the *cakras* (the subtle spiritual centers) along the spine and in the brain. Not only did She draw figures of the *cakras* but She explained in detail their functioning during man's spiritual advance. Years later Bhāijī compared Ānandamayī Mā's drawings of the *cakras* with those found in Sir John George Woodroffe's *Serpent Power* and found that they were in agreement. When he wanted to show the book to Ānandamayī Mā, She did not even look at it. Instead the illiterate Ānandamayī Mā revealed to him details about the *cakras* not known to the western scholar.*

Gradually, the unusual phenomena in Ānandamayī Mā's life receded into the background. The "*sādhanā*" phase was over by the end of 1926. Even before that Ānandamayī Mā or Mā (mother in Bengali) or Mātājī (mother in Hindi) as She was called by Her devotees, had extended the field of Her activity beyond the Dacca area. She embarked upon travels throughout East Bengal and even all over Northern India.

In May, 1926, for instance, She visited the temple sites of Deogarh in Bihar at the request of Her devotee Prān Gopal Mukherji, the former Deputy Postmaster General of Dacca, who had retired to Deogarh to live there close to the āśram of his guru, Balānanda Brahmachari Maharaj. Mukherji introduced Mā to Balānanda. The renowned sage was deeply impressed by Her and exclaimed that he regarded Her as the Divine Mother incarnate. Through Balānanda other *mahātmās*

* For Ānandamayī Mā's description of the *cakras*, see Appendix III.

(great souls) flocked to Her. Wherever She went from now on She attracted magnetlike the saints and sages of India. Soon after Her return from Deogarh, She ceased to cover Her face with the folds of Her sari. Her whole being now exuded confidence, so that people felt the urge to bring their spiritual problems to Her. The counseling phase of Her life was under way.

Early in 1927 Ānandamayī Mā and Her entourage visited the sacred pilgrimage centers of Hrishikesh and Hardwar in the Himalayas. While in Hardwar She ordered Didi and her father to stay there for three months and practise *sādhanā* in solitude. She had decided that the time had come to eradicate whatever worldly traits were still lingering in those two close devotees. In the austere simplicity of the Himalayas they were to live a life of renunciation. Considering that Sasanka Mohan Mukherjee was an elderly man and that he was used to comforts (for Indian circumstances), he showed remarkable hardiness. He had to get accustomed to walking long distances over rugged terrain and to bathing in cold streams. The spiritual path is not meant for weaklings. The bliss permeated Mother, meanwhile, continued Her travels, stopping at Mathura and Vrindaban, the sites of Lord Kṛṣṇa's earthly *līlā*, and Vārāṇasi the spiritual capital of India, before returning to Dacca.

The devotees in Dacca were gradually becoming aware of the fact that their monopoly on Mā was a matter of the past. Ever more frequently did She go on extended trips. In July, 1927, Her *kheyāla* prompted Her to go to Vindhyācal in Uttar Pradesh. At that time Vindhyācal consisted of a few huts in the midst of a jungle. When they reached Vindhyācal, Ānandamayī Mā walked around as though in a trance. She explained that it was hallowed ground, permeated by the vibrations of numerous saints of former ages. The government was notified that it ought to undertake excavations in the region of Vindhyācal. Eventually several temple ruins were uncovered precisely where Mā had sensed an especially holy atmosphere. Vindhyācal became one of Her favourite sites for retreats. An āśram was erected there, serving as another link in the chain of centers animated by Ānandamayī Mā's spirituality.

In April, 1927, on the occasion of Ānandamayī Mā's thirty-first birthday, Bhāijī suggested that special *kīrtana* and *pūjā* be performed in Her honour. Henceforth elaborate birthday celebrations have been regularly held, lasting over a week and attended by large crowds. Some may wonder why the egoless Ānandamayī Mā, who is beyond time and space, permits the celebration of Her birthdays. After all, according to the *Bhagavad Gītā*: "Nor I, nor thou, nor any one of these, ever was not, nor ever will not be." On Her sixtieth birthday commemoration, in 1956, when a devotee asked Her about the meaning of Her birthday, She replied that it was true that She was not born, nor was Lord Kṛṣṇa for that matter, and yet His birthday is being celebrated. Such birthdays, consisting entirely of religious functions, serve to focus people's attention on the divine and thereby increase their devotion and spiritual receptivity.

Bhāijī was not only responsible for initiating special birthday functions for Mā but he also made chants to "Mā" an integral part of *kīrtanas* in Her āśrams:[1] "Merge all names and forms in the 'Mā' *mantra*, Say always Mā, Mā, and let your eyes swim in floods of tears, Find in Śrī Ānandamayī Mā the final refuge of your life's journey," was one of the chants composed by Bhāijī.

Three months after the celebration of Her thirty-first birthday, on 3rd August, 1927, the bliss permeated Mother, visited Her birthplace, Kheorā, accompanied by Bholānāth and Her mother, normally referred to as Didima (grand-mother). Their erstwhile home had been sold to Moslems who had changed it almost beyond recognition, so that Didimā found it difficult to orient herself in it. Ānandamayī Mā, however, went straight to an enclosure where cow dung was kept and identified it as the spot where She had been born. Then something totally unexpected happened. She picked up a piece of earth from that very site while tears were flooding Her eyes. How is one to interpret this show of emotion coming from the evenminded Ānandamayī Mā who, as a rule, is detached from life and death, joy and sorrow? May be this behaviour will appear less puzzling, if we keep in mind that, according to Hindu philosophy, God is both in and beyond manifestation; thus while He is beyond duality, He also manifests as duality. It is also known that the great *avatāras*

1. See also p. 71.

voluntarily take on human limitations. Perhaps, at this juncture of Her *līlā*, Ānandamayī Mā saw fit to play the role of a common mortal with emotional attachment to Her place of birth which She had not seen for seventeen years. One must also bear in mind that Ānandamayī Mā already knew that She would soon leave Her homeland, Beṇgal, where She would return for brief visits only. She may have wanted to give Her devotees advance notice of the impending change and chose a symbolic gesture for this purpose.

Early in 1928 Bholānāth lost his job in Shah-bagh. For the time being, whenever they were not travelling, Ānandamayī Mā, Bholānāth, Her parents and Aunt Mātari rented a house in the Tikatuli district of Dacca. In September, 1928, during a visit to Vārāṇasi, She met Mahāmahopādhyāya Gopināth Kavirāj, one of India's greatest Sanskrit scholars, then Principal of Queen's College in Vārāṇasi. He became one of Her foremost devotees and is responsible for many publications about Ānandamayī Mā. At Vārāṇasi Mā was practically inundated by crowds of *darśana* seekers. Whatever had remained of Her "private" life was swallowed up by Her duties to those who sought spiritual solace from Her. Bholānāth had to adjust himself to a life that included few of the normal aspects of a householder's existence. In December, 1928, Ānandamayī Mā decided that the time had come to intensify Bholānāth's *sādhanā*. She told him to go for solitary meditation to Tārāpeeth, a sacred site whose cremation grounds are ideally suited for yogic practices.

The temporary absence of Bholānāth raised the question who was to "look after" Ānandamayī Mā. One still felt the need to uphold certain properties. How could a woman be without a guardian ? It was decided to designate Didi's father as Her "guardian". Although She was recognized to be a great saint, if not the Divine Mother in the flesh, She still was subject to certain restrictions as a woman. Obviously holiness did not entirely make up for a woman's inferior status. Many men admitted that they initially had to face the taunts of their relatives for sitting at the feet of a mere woman.

Whatever their relatives might say, devotees of Ānandamayī Mā could not resist the magnetism of Her personality. When Her birthday was celebrated in May 1929, the Siddheśvarī āśram was found inadequate to accommodate all Her followers. The celebrations were therefore held at the newly completed āśram in Ramna. At the end of the birthday ceremonies Ānandamayī Mā abruptly announced that She would leave Dacca that very night. Bholānāth was to stay at Ramna āśram. In conformity with Her role as an obedient wife, She asked Bholānāth's permission to leave, although She made it unmistakably clear that permission had to be granted: "If you say, 'no', I shall leave this body at your feet just now." She was amenable, however, to Bholānāth's request that She travel in the company of Her father. Otherwise: "People will speak ill of you..," he had pleaded.

Ānandamayī Mā left Ramna around midnight by the next available train which took Her to Mymensingh in East Bengal. From there She travelled to Cox Bazar (East Bengal) and then to Hardwar, Dehradun (in the Himalayas), Ayodhya (Uttar Pradesh) and Vārāṇāsi. She did not inform Bholānāth about Her moves. Shortly after Her return to Dacca, She was no longer able to hold on to kitchen utensils and consequently had to relinquish all household work. This new development was more than Bholānāth was willing to bear. After all, he was still very human. Feelings of frustration had accumulated by that time. In addition, his relatives urged him at long last to assert his position as head of the household. He mustered all his courage and remonstrated with Ānandamayī Mā. What ensued is best described in Her own words: "I tried to cook for a few days with mother's help... I had no objections and it made no difference to me... (but) Bholānāth fell ill after a few days, and then I myself was ill. So it did not after all come to anything at all." Evidently the household *līlā* was over, while Bholānāth's education continued.

Not only was Bholānāth deprived of Her cooking skills, he had to give up one more physical comfort which he had so far still enjoyed: sleeping in a bed. Some time in October, 1929, when Ānandamayī Mā was again in poor health, She made him leave his bed in the middle of the night, ostensibly because She wanted to occupy it. He had to lie on the floor in a blanket, the way She was wont to sleep. This more austere mode of sleeping became a permanent arrangement for Bholānāth, for within a few days Ānandamayī Mā had his bed taken apart while She returned to sleeping on the floor.

At the time when Ānandamayī Mā was further disciplining Bholānāth, She experienced Her first encounter with the academic community. When a congress of Indian philosophers was convened in Dacca in 1929, some of the delegates visited Ānandamayī Mā. For hours the uneducated Mā answered spontaneously the most profound questions thrown at Her by the erudite scholars. Her "reputation" was firmly established and members of the learned professions came to Her in increasing numbers. There followed a period of travels seemingly at random all over northern India. Then, in August, 1930, Mā ventured on Her first visit to Southern India, all the way to Cape Comorin. Although She did not speak any of the South Indian languages, She was received with reverence wherever She travelled. She showed great fascination for the vastly different culture of the South and gave occasional hints that She was quite "at home" in South India, that She was on familiar ground.*

One more birthday was celebrated in Dacca in May/June 1932. Previously, whenever She had left Dacca, She had assured Her devotees that She would return to that city. But on the night of June 2, 1932, She informed Didi about Her intention to leave Dacca permanently. Any attempt to dissuade Her from Her plan would be in vain: "Let me move about according to my *kheyāla*. I cannot do so if you all put obstacles in my path." At 11.30 p.m. She had Bhāijī summoned. Except for Bholānāth he was the only one to accompany Her. Bhāijī had to make a momentous decision. He realized that following Ānandamayī Mā meant severing his family ties. He pleaded for time to fetch money from his home but was told that they would leave immediately. With hardly any baggage the three departed from Dacca. True renunciation is clearly not compatible with concern for worldly ballast. At the railroad station Ānandamayī Mā asked for tickets "right up to the terminus of the line," which happened to be Jagannathgunj. From there they proceeded to the Himalayas. Uninterrupted travelling followed. Only towards the end of 1935 did Ānandamayī Mā

* Only in 1952 did Mā tour the South again. During the second visit She had a brief meeting with "the Mother" of the Sri Aurobindo Ashram in Pondicherry.

Prime Minister Jawaharlal Nehru has Ma's darśana at Her New Delhi Ashram.

revisit Dacca for four days. Like "a bird on the wing" She has been travelling ever since, staying only for a few days, at most a few weeks, at any one place. "I find one vast garden spread out all over the universe. All plants, all human beings, all higher mind-bodies are about in this garden in various ways, each has its own uniqueness and beauty. Their presence and variety give me great delight. Everyone of you adds with his special feature to the glory of the garden. I move about from one place to another in the same garden. What makes you feel my absence so keenly when I happen to leave your part of the garden for another, to gladden your brothers over there ?" Wherever She goes *kīrtanas* and *pūjās* are celebrated. The focus is always on the divine.

While originally Ānandamayī Mā spoke only Bengali, She gradually acquired facility in Hindi. Although there remains an inner core of Bengali devotees, many non-Bengali Indians and even foreigners can now be counted among Her devotees. Followers include businessmen, artists, scholars, journalists, *mahātmās*, rājās and rānīs as well as government leaders. Already in 1933 Kamala Nehru, the wife of Jawarharlal Nehru, visited Her in Dehradun. From that time on Kamala frequently saw Ānandamayī Mā and meditated in Her presence. The bliss permeated Mother was extremely gracious to Her. Many years later, reminiscing about Kamala, Ānandamayī Mā revealed that Kamala had had exceptionally deep meditations and had been repeatedly blessed with visions of Kṛṣna. It was through Kamala Nehru's inspiration that She had requested all Her devotees to set aside at least fifteen minutes daily for divine communion. When Kamala became seriously ill, the bliss permeated Mother visited her several times in the hospital near Almora. After Kamala's death, a rosary (*japa mālā*) given to Her by Ānandamayī Mā, was handed on to Her daughter, Indira Gandhi, who treasures it to this day. Indira Gandhi as well as Her father Jawarharlal Nehru continued to visit Ānandamayī Mā. Her duties as Prime Minister of India do not keep Indira from seeking Mā's *darśana*. Her mother Kamala was also instrumental in bringing together Mahatma Gandhi and Ānandamayī Mā. Several meetings ensued. Once Mā participated in one of Gandhiji's prayer meetings. Other well-known Indian devotees include the former President of India, Rajendra

Prasad, and the former Vice-President Gopal Svarup Pathak, the former Chief Justice of Mysore, Subdharanjan Dasgupta, Vijayaraje, Maharani of Gwalior, the wealthy industrialist and philanthropist, Jugal Kishore Birla, the singer Dilip Kumar Roy, the dancer Uday Shankar, Professors Tripurari Chakravarti of Calcutta University, Bireshwar Ganguly of Patna University, and Raihana Tyabji, a Moslem woman saint, who was close to Gandhiji.

Among the foreigners who were attracted to Ānandamayī Mā is an Austrian who eventually became a renunciant and is now known under the name of Brahmacārinī Ātmānanda. When she met Ānandamayī Mā, she only knew some colloquial Hindi. Gradually she acquired a perfect knowledge of Bengali and has been instrumental in translating Ānandamayī Mā's teaching into English. Dr. Adolphe Jacques Weintrob, a successful medical practitioner from Marseille, has become Brahmacāri Vijayānanda and lived upon Ānandamayī Mā's instruction in seclusion in Almora for several years and is now at Kankhal. The well-known British photographer Richard Lannoy, the French film producer, Arnaud Desjardins, and the German novelist, Melita Maschmann, also found that Ānandamayī Mā was the answer to their spiritual longings. Melita Maschmann published a book about her impressions of Ānandamayī Mā under the title, *Der Tiger singt Kirtana.* It is a spiritual masterpiece, showing the great sensitivity of the German writer. An Italian woman, Miriam Orr, became a devotee of Ānandamayī Mā immediately upon seeing a photograph of the bliss permeated Mother. In recent years Mā has been visited by the Swiss and Chilean ambassadors, the Queen Mother of Greece and the Canadian Prime Minister, Trudeau.

From 1932 to the present Ānandamayī Mā's *līlā* has been an uninterrupted outpouring of divine counsel, an incessant call to mankind to awaken from the sleep of delusion to the realization of the One who alone is real. The conventional historian will be utterly frustrated by Her unconcern for worldly events. But, after all, is not history the epitome of *māyā* ? Thus Gandhiji's non-violent campaign, the independence struggle, the Partition of India are almost totally ignored by Her. She only briefly commented upon the Punjab massacres in 1947, simply stating that they happened because they were bound to happen. When Gandhiji was assassinated She likened his death to Christ's crucifixion. Apart from these two instances, there are no references to political events. Melita Maschmann provides us with a clue to Ānandamayī Mā's apparent disregard of political events. The German novelist stayed with the bliss permeated Mother during the Cuban missile crisis of 1961. She relates that she was able to retain her calmness throughout the crisis, even though she was aware of the danger inherent in the situation. Being in the presence of Mā helped her to raise her consciousness above the realm of duality, and made her realize that her true Self cannot be touched by anything material. Where bliss reigns, fear must vanish.

Instead of "significant" historical landmarks, Ānandamayī Mā's *līlā* from 1932 to the present constitutes an unending procession of religious festivals, *kīrtanas* and *satsangas*. And the bliss permeated Mother continues to roam all over Northern India surrounded by some of Her closest followers and eagerly awaited by thousands of devotees who hope to benefit from Her presence. Of course, some of those who used to accompany the Mother are no longer with Her. In 1937 Bhāijī joined Ānandamayī Mā on a pilgrimage to Mount Kailāsh, the mythical abode of Lord Śiva. On the way Bhāijī was suddenly overcome by an urge for complete renunciation. Ānandamayī Mā spontaneously uttered mantras accompanying *saṁnyāsa* initiation and bestowed upon him the monastic name Swami Mounānanda Parvat. A few days following his initiation he contracted a fever and died in Almora with the words "Mā, Mā" on his lips. Bholānāth died of small pox in 1938. Two years earlier, in 1936, Ānandamayī Mā's father had passed on. His wife, Didimā, became a renunciant under the name of Swāmi Muktānanda Giri in 1939. Since Ānandamayī Mā does not consider Herself a guru, She frequently asked Her mother to initiate aevotees. Indefatigably Didimā served at her daughter's side until her death at the age of ninety-three, on August 8th, 1970.

Since the number of Ānandamayī Mā's followers had tremendously increased over the years and new āśrams had sprung up across northern and central India, a regular organization was needed for administrative purposes. In February, 1950, the Shree Shree Ānandamayee Sangha was established in Vārāṇasi with the following objectives: (1) to promote methods aiming at

Self-realization, (2) to start centers for practising *sādhanā*, (3) to organize religious functions, (4) to give free medical relief to deserving persons and provide financial and medical assistance to sādhus and brahmacāris. The bliss permeated Mother is in no way involved in the management or control of the Shree Shree Ānandamayee Sangha. Its governing body consists of forty-one members while the day to day activities are supervised by an executive council of ten. Contributions from laymen are its only source of revenue. The Sangha has established two institutions in which a balanced spiritual, mental and physical education is provided for boys and girls separately. Since 1952, a quarterly journal Ānanda Vārtā has been published, in Bengali, Hindi and English. In its pages one can find not only Ānandamayī Mā's teaching and news about Her but also spiritually uplifting articles on all religions. In 1965 a modern hospital has been founded in Vārāṇasi providing free treatment for destitute persons.

Although Ānandamayī Mā has shown relatively little concern for institutions devoted to man's material welfare, She did attend the opening of the hospital and gave Her blessings to its functioning. The institution for which She personally is responsible, however, is the annual *Samyam Vrata* (vow of self-restraint, self-control), started in 1952. She is well aware of the fact that modern men, even in India, are deeply enmeshed in worldly activities and rarely willing to live a life of total renunciation. Knowing that "the world is too much with us," She wants the lay devotees to abandon worldly living for at least one week each year and to devote that time entirely to spiritual pursuits. The *Samyam Vratas* take place each year in a different location, either in āśrams or on grounds provided for that purpose by wealthy devotees. Participants vow to fast except for one light meal a day and to abstain from quarrelling, gossiping, smoking, drinking tea and coffee (not to speak of alcohol) and sex during that week. Everyone lives in utmost simplicity, sometimes in tents. Pandits and *Mahātmās* address the "renunciants for a week" during the day. At night Ānandamayī Mā holds *satsanga* for about an hour. Some time is spent in *kīrtana* and collective meditation. Several hundred people, including a few westerners, attend the *Samyam Vratas* as a rule. One devotee appropriately called the *Samyam Vratas* "spiritual training grounds." They may be regarded as beacons at a time when the majority of men are enveloped in a darkness created by their material-mindedness. The bliss permeated Mother considers them building blocs for a new society, a society whose primary concern is not the accumulation of material wealth but God-realization.

By urging mankind to renounce the world for one week, Ānandamayī Mā is asking them to practise only an infinitesimal fraction of that renunciation which has been Her way of life for half a century. She has no home and in spite of Her advanced age continues to be "a bird on the wing". All the gifts that are showered upon Her leave Her indifferent and are often immediately distributed to others.

At the time of writing the bliss permeated Mother is in Her seventy-seventh year. Naturally, time has left its mark on Her body. Her health leaves much to be desired from a normal worldly "human" point of view. Ānandamayī Mā, however, remains undisturbed: "For this body there is no cause whatever for inconvenience or discomfort. This (ill-health) is also a fine play. This body observes in minute detail what is taking place in its every nerve and vein...For this body, everything without exception is but a play...Whatever be the *kheyāla* at any particular moment, according to that, things may happen." So, in sickness or health She goes on, a constant reminder to all of us that we too should strive to attain a state beyond duality where no physical suffering can touch us.

CHAPTER II

PERSONALITY AND TEACHINGS OF ĀNANDAMAYĪ MĀ

How is one to deal with the personality of someone who defies all categorization, so dear to the western analytic mind ? Her devotees to this day wonder who She really is. Learned disquisitions have been written analyzing various possibilities. Is She a God-intoxicated mystic ? Is She an *avatāra* ? Is She the Absolute Itself ?..Is She a manifestation of the Divine Mother ? The Italian devotee Miriam Orr, concludes: "Mother is not a human being like all the others. She is Divine Light clad in a human form." No attempt will be made in this study to decide who the bliss permeated Mother really is. It may be useful though to elaborate on the Mother aspect of Ānandamayī Mā. While in the west God is thought of as Father, in India many revere the Divine in the form of the Mother. In Bengal especially Mother Kālī or Mother Durgā have been venerated since ancient times. Bengal's great novelist, Bankim Candra Chatterjee, composed the hymn "Bande Mātaram" (Hail to the Mother) which inspired Bengalis during their freedom struggle against the British in the first decade of the twentieth century and which eventually became a national song of all India. Undoubtedly Ānandamayī Mā possesses a specific motherly appeal. Some of Her closest devotees who had lost their own mother found that Anandamayī Mā fulfilled their need for a mother, but in a way no ordinary human being would be able to do.

Can we obtain a clue to Her identity from the bliss permeated Mother Herself ? Naturally She has been frequently asked to reveal Herself. At one occasion She stated: "From your worldly standpoint this body belongs to East Bengal and is a Brahmin by caste; but if you think apart from these artificial distinctions, you will understand that this body is one of the members of one human family." If we consider that all verbal expressions are by their very nature limited, the closest approximation to truth about Ānandamayī Mā seems to be contained in Her answer: "Well, I am what you consider me to be, not more, not less." Or: "This body is like a musical instrument;

what you hear depends upon how you play it." Is it not rather striking that although many a skilled photographer has tried his hand at taking Her picture, each photograph has turned out distinctly different. One is tempted to conclude that we are witnessing in Her "person" the infinitely varying aspects of the cosmos. Under those circumstances, our vision of Ānandamayī Mā will even fall short of the description rendered by the legendary six blind boys who washed different parts of an elephant's body and produced six distinct accounts of how the elephant looks. It will depend upon our state of consciousness, to what extent we shall be able to fathom the phenomenon called Ānandamayī Mā.

There seems to be general agreement that She does not exhibit what is normally considered ego consciousness. No personal likes or dislikes, cravings or aversions are apparent. At no time did She have to face the agonizing struggles, conflicts, temptations and doubts occurring in the lives of even the greatest saints. She is totally devoid of fear and anger. Whenever She displays moods it is clear that She is acting in that manner to bring home a certain point, to teach a lesson. Instead of being the captive of common human motivations and impulses, She follows what She terms *kheyāla.* Ordinarily it means spontaneous action, or even caprice, but the way Ānandamayī Mā employs it to explain Her own actions and behaviour as well as that of God or the Absolute, it is best translated as 'divine will,' with the implication that it is not subject to the normal cause and effect process. It is thus entirely free from any conditioning. Ānandamayī Mā's "decisions" to stay in one place or another, to cure one person but not another, Her reaction to various *darśana* seekers with kindness, severity, indifference or attentiveness, are all explained by Her as the result of *kheyāla.* For example. She visited Dr. Gopināth Kavirāj in June 1961 while he was lying in a hospital in Bombay. On the way out She had the *kheyāla* to stop at the bed of a Moslem patient who was dying from cancer. She stroked all over his body blessing him. Obviously there were many other deadly sick patients, but Her *kheyāla* singled him out. Once She stunned Her devotees by greeting with laughter a disciple who had just suffered the loss of his wife. Offended by Her seemingly callous attitude, he asked Her for the cause of Her merriment. "Pitājī" (an endearment of father), She replied, "There is one less barrier between you and God." On the other hand, Ānandamayī Mā can act kindly beyond human comprehension. A young man had terribly misbehaved while staying in one of Her āśrams. He was most egotistic and stubborn, driving the other āśram inmates to desperation. They finally told Ānandamayī Mā that he ought to be expelled from the āśram. But She replied "When nobody wants such a poor and hapless boy, don't you think that he needs me most ? Will it do you and the world any good if this perverse young man be allowed to rot in the mire ?" The young misfit stayed and in time became one of Her finest devotees.

As Her name indicates, She is considered the very incarnation of bliss. Even now, although She is advanced in years, Her pealing laughter is infectious. Seeing Her one realizes the truth proclaimed by the Taittirīya Upaniṣad: "From joy springs the universe." Countless are the humorous stories and incidents from Her life which She enjoys telling in the intimate circle of Her close devotees. Once some devotees dressed Her as the boy Krishna and She became identified with the youthful prank-loving god. She is completely in tune with nature. During a boat trip to Cox Bazar in East Bengal, a tremendous storm erupted. Most passengers were panicky with fear, but Ānandamayī Mā enjoyed the spectacle. Looking at the tossing waves She remarked: "Listen to the uninterrupted *kīrtana* that is going on over there." Just as does Lord Siva in the form of *Naṭarāja*, the Cosmic Dancer, She experiences the thrill of the cosmic play, be it ever so destructive. It is true that occasionally She shows signs of exhaustion, especially after a celebration in Calcutta, where thousands upon thousands of devotees pass by Her, offering garlands to Her, which She returns to them with a blessing. There are times when She experiences sickness, but, as has been pointed out earlier, She accepts all bodily discomfort with equanimity. Being anchored in the one Reality, why should She reject this essential aspect of delusive manifestation ? It too gives Her joy, She avers. Once, after She had been seriously ill in August, 1929, She explained: "This body moves in tune with nature, its natural course must have somehow been thwarted in its normal functioning," indicating that Her devotees had attempted to interfere with Her *kheyāla*.

Her followers claim that She is continuously in the highest state of *samādhi*. Even as She looks at you, you are aware of the fact that She is with you and yet far beyond you; that She has that dual vision encompassing the manifest and the transcendent. In Her presence one feels as though mentally stripped naked. There is no point in trying to hide anything. As uncomfortable as this may appear to be, it is tempered by the realization that Ānandamayī Mā understands all and does not condemn anyone, for from Her point of view you are, above all, a soul, possibly greatly tarnished by egoistic tendencies, but still a soul. Being in Her presence produces a consciousness of one's imperfections as well as an extreme feeling of serenity. Even a beginner on the spiritual path will sense that he is in intimate contact with the divine, especially if he has the privilege to be present during one of those occasions when She chants, to the accompaniment of a harmonium, either "*He Bhagavān* !. (O, Lord)," or "*Satyam, Jñānam, Anantam, Brahma* (Truth, wisdom, infinite, absolute)". Her voice has remained youthful even though Her body is aging. Her chanting sweeps aside all earthly attachments, and, at least temporarily, one feels in tune with the One. The quintessence of Her being is summed up in the statement—"The most remarkable characteristic of Mā Ānandamayī . . is to awaken or intensify the keen desire for the spiritual life in all who approach Her."

While Ānandamayī Mā refuses to be considered a guru, She cannot escape being constantly approached for spiritual guidance. For all practical purposes She does have disciples, even though they may not have received formal initiation from Her. And She is ever ready to teach by Her very being, by Her actions and by direct counseling. Warning people not to depend on book learning, She teaches in a simple, homely language, often by means of parables, just as did Ramakrishna. She is particularly fond of punning, for which Bengali is well suited. Thus Vedānta (monistic Indian philosophy) means *bheda anta* (end of difference); where Rāma (God) is, there is ārāma (rest); where Rāma is not, there is *byārāma* (discomfort, disease); desire (*vāsanā*) is where God does not dwell (*vāsa nā*); *sādhanā* has to be practised to discover *svā dhana* (one's own wealth).*

* In Bengali *sādhana* and *svā dhana* have the almost identical pronunciation.

Frequently She does not offer specific advice. Instead She points out various ways of viewing a problem. For instance, someone asked Her whether it was proper for him to engage in a suit, in view of the fact that he had been cheated in a business deal. In reply, She stated that one could argue that one must go to court to teach the culprit a lesson and to keep him from further crime. On the other hand, who is really cheating ?: "Are not all forms, all beings manifestations of Him ? What I have been deprived of was evidently not my due. It is God who has taken it from me." Another way of looking at the problem is that through generosity and forgiveness one might bring about a transformation in the criminal. Or one might refrain from going to court, considering it sufficient punishment that the villain had caused bad karma for himself. Finally, one could reason that one would not go to court if the wrongdoer were one's own brother. "Whichever of these points of view appeals to you, according to it you should act."

When someone complained to Ānandamayī Mā about Her unwillingness to give clear-cut answers to problems, She retorted: "At least you have understood that there is a state where problems are no longer settled in any particular way...no solution is ever conclusive..The resolution of a problem arrived at by the mind must of necessity be from a particular point of view; consequently there will be room for contradiction, since your solution represents but one aspect." Only by transcending the region of multifacedness can one arrive at *the* one solution.

Ānandamayī Mā uses every possible occasion to teach. At Her āśram in Solon, for instance, the entrance is guarded by two wooden tigers. They have been so realistically painted that they appear as though they are on the verge of pouncing upon any potential prey. Once when a dog came to the āśram to beg for food, Ānandamayī Mā placed some food close to the wooden tigers. The dog obviously was in a quandary He was eager to eat the food but fear of the tigers kept him from touching it. Ānandamayī Mā thereupon jokingly remarked that the dog found himself in the position of most human beings who are held captive by their imaginary fears.

Directly or indirectly Ānandamayī Mā works on those who have entrusted their lives to Her guidance to rid themselves of imperfections. Vijayānanda (Dr. Weintrob) relates that he had shown undue concern about finding seating accommodations for himself during their frequent travels—anyone knowing how overcrowded Indian trains are will sympathize with his weakness. Craving for material comforts, however, is an obstacle to spiritual advancement. Once Vijayānanda had just figured out exactly how he could obtain for himself a desirable seat and had taken up an advantageous position on the station platform. His shrewd calculation was unfortunately upset by Ānandamayī Mā. When the train pulled into the station, She asked him to take care of a big assortment of baggage and to see to it that it be safely put on the train. It was a drastic lesson in overcoming selfishness. Apparently he learnt that lesson quickly, for, as a "reward" Ānandamayī Mā saw to it that he did get a suitable seat. Vijayānanda also tells us that the bliss permeated Mother can be most persistent in pointing out over and over again specific shortcomings of Her devotees, such as loss of temper, quarrelsomeness or tendency to gossip, right in front of other devotees. Vijayānanda relates that he had used intemperate language towards one of the āśram inmates in Mā's presence. He almost immediately regretted his loss of self-control and asked Her forgiveness in private, hoping that this obviously minor matter would thereby be laid at rest. However, Ānandamayī Mā questioned all those concerned in the incident in a most elaborate manner, dwelling on it for what seemed an undue amount of time. Later Vijayānanda came to understand that it was Her method to eradicate thoroughly whatever shortcoming may prove a hindrance in one's spiritual progress. By paying exceptional attention to his minor failing and examining it in detail, She made him aware of the underlying cause for his flare-up, some pentup emotion. Before long he was able to overcome this imperfection.

Like the Divine Mother She can be exceedingly compassionate at one time and seemingly cruel at another, whatever approach is deemed necessary to free Her charges from delusion. Her teaching is always adjusted to the needs of the individual and varies in accordance with his or her religious background. It does not matter whether one is a monist, dualist, Moslem, Buddhist or Christian. Ānandamayī Mā has the ability to attune Herself to the particular religious point of view and the level of understanding of those who consult Her. Vijayānanda observes: "A vedāntist, for example, when talking to Mother for the first time, will feel convinced that She is a pure *advaita* (non-dualist) vedāntin; a *śakta* (worshipper of the Divine Mother) may very likely say that She is an incarnation of the Divine Mother, advocating the cult of *śakti*; while a *vaiṣṇava* will see in Her a great *bhakta* (follower of the devotional path). It is only after having known Her fairly closely and for a long time that one becomes aware of Her innumerable facets." Arnaud Desjardins reported that Ānandamayī Ma brought him closer to Christ. Buddhists, Sikhs and Moslems find that She strengthens their faith in their respective beliefs. The gist of Ānandamayī Mā's message is that only One (God, Brahman) truly exists: "The One who is the Eternal the Ātman (true Self), He Himself is the traveller on the path of Immortality. He is all in all, He alone is." Everything else is nothing but an elaboration of this statement, just a commentary. Thus, in the ultimate sense, one may consider Her a monist, provided one understands that dualism is a facet of monism, for it is the One that seeks expression in infinite varieties of forms, ways and events. It is the One that is engaged in the *līlā* of creation, preservation and destruction. It is the One that is deeply involved in every aspect of the *līlā* and yet is beyond the *līlā*. Actually He (the One) plays hide and seek with Himself. Absolute oneness makes a *līlā* impossible. So, to enjoy the *līlā*, the One has created the veil of separateness (*māyā*) as a disguise, but we must not forget that He Himself is also the disguise. He is playing blindman's buff with Himself. He is disguised as manifoldness, variety, relativity. Often Ānandamayī Mā uses the analogy of water or the ocean to explain how One can have different aspects. By varying the temperature, one can turn water into ice or steam, without changing its essential nature. Similarly, stormy weather can temporarily divide an ocean into individual waves but when calm returns, the waves merge into the Ocean. All come from One and return to One.'

To give an illustration of God's game of hide and seek, Ānandamayī Mā tells the following story. A wealthy merchant once went on a business trip. A thief in the disguise of a businessman joined him, intent upon robbing him at the earliest suitable occasion. Every morning, before leaving the inn in which they happened to have put up for the night, the merchant would count his money quite openly and then put it into his pocket. At night the merchant went to sleep seemingly without suspicion. While he was asleep the thief would frantically search through all the belongings of the merchant without being able to find the money. After several nights of frustrating searching, the thief finally in resignation confessed to the merchant his true intention and pleaded with him to tell him how he was able to hide his money so successfully. The merchant replied casually: "I knew from the beginning what you were up to. So, every night I placed the money under your pillow. I could safely sleep, knowing fully well that that would be the one place where you would never look." And Ānandamayī Mā comments: "God is within everyone, but man goes out in search of Him. This is what constitutes God's Play and God's Creation."

Unity in variety also applies to the religious realm. Just as individual human beings have been created with various tendencies, abilities, temperaments, so religious paths have come about in response to different religious needs. Men may dispute which is the ideal path, but when the goal of Oneness is reached, all quarrelling ceases, for quarrelling presupposes alternatives, distinctions. Holding such a view Ānandamayī Mā, while showing utmost respect for Christianity, unequivocally rejects Christianity's claim to the one true religion. How dare anyone assume that the *infinite* Lord would provide only one path of salvation.

Irrespective of which religious path one embraces, the aim of religion must be to pierce through the veil of delusion to discover the underlying Oneness, and ultimately to merge with the One. This is the foremost, nay, the only duty of man. This is what distinguishes man from all other creatures. "...it is man's duty to bear in mind that he exists for God alone—for His service and for the realization of Him." Finding the One is the cure-all for all worldly sufferings and human imperfections. For how is it possible to show hostility towards anyone or anything when one knows that all beings and all things are interrelated and essentially one. Then and only then does it become possible to accept, even welcome all of life's experiences, be they ever so painful. It must have been this unitary view that enabled St. Francis to welcome sickness and death, to feel kinship with all life including Brother Fire and Sister Sun.

Why the many exist and why this *līlā* is going on cannot really be explained in finite terms. The One who is beyond time and space is equally beyond cause and effect which are aspects of delusion. Thus the question "why ?" is itself a facet of *māyā*. The mind which operates on the basis of time and space, cause and effect, is in no way able to grasp ultimate Reality. Consequently, only when one has personally experienced Oneness, i.e. transcended multiplicity, will one be able to know ultimate truth, a truth that is beyond the "why". This world is a world of contradictions and no sense can be made of it as long as one is involved in it. But it is our good fortune that the One who has created the veil of delusion has also provided us with the ways and means to annihilate delusion. And it is delusion itself that eventually becomes the means for overcoming delusion.

Being deluded, man believes that this world of duality is real, and that he can find happiness in it. But the world has been so constructed that it cannot provide real i.e., lasting happiness. The word world (*jagat* movement) gives the clue to its nature. It is constant movement, perpetual change, coming and going, health and sickness, fame and disgrace, richness and poverty, birth and death. No permanent contentment, no peace "that passeth understanding" can be expected in this world. Man must realize that it is not his true home: "When one resides in a country not one's own, how can one possibly evade the hardships that are a foreigner's lot ? Your Motherland is where there is no question of distress and sorrow, of violence and hatred, of estrangement, neither of the opposites of light and darkness." Being an alien, a visitor, man must not tarry here unduly. As long as he in his ignorance believes that he can find happiness here, whether in the form of fame, richness, power, human love, he will, upon death, have to return to this world for further lessons. His earthly attachments will automatically provide him with a "return ticket" as Ānandmayī Mā so fittingly describes it.

Since Ānandamayī Mā urges man to start upon the return trip to the One, does She imply that man has free will successfully to undertake the journey by his own efforts ? As we well know, theologians across the centuries have disputed this thorny question. She makes it clear that there is a subtle interrelationship between free will and grace, free will being in the ultimate sense a part of grace, as contradictory as this may sound. Thus

She states: "Verily, everything in the world is achieved by will-power. If by determination and patience someone can translate his ideal into life, his actions will be inspired. Such a worker is backed by Divine Power." As long as we are in ignorance, we are seemingly free in minor matters only. Our weaknesses, our inadequacies bind us. We are the slaves of our moods, cravings and impulses. Ānandamayī Mā likens the average man's freedom to that of a cow which is tied by a rope to a post. Within the limits of the rope she has freedom. But, of course, were the cow able to break loose from the rope, she would gain complete freedom. Similarly, the person who makes the right spiritual effort can cut thereby the rope of delusion that binds him to the finite world of pseudo-happiness and attain freedom. It is true that ordinarily the law of karma operates in the universe. Accordingly man "reaps as he sows," not necessarily in one life time. Eventually, however, karma catches up with him. Since all beings interact with each other, all actions, thoughts and feelings make their imprint upon this universe. The universe can be likened to a vast computer into which all actions, thoughts and feelings are fed. The computer then converts those actions, thoughts and feelings into consequences whose effect will be experienced by us at a specific time and in a specific form depending on the result of the interplay between the various "inputs". Thus all accrued karma is bound to ripen into fruition at the proper time.

Over and over again Ānandamayī Mā states: "All that occurs, good or bad,—if it was predestined to happen—comes about through the mysterious working together of certain forces," or "Whatever happens was destined to happen."

The bliss permeated Mother is, however, by no means a strict predestinarian. The law of karma is not the only factor to be considered, for God is not bound by any laws. His free will prevails over man's seemingly free will. To illustrate this point She uses the following analogy. A man who has planted flowers in his garden may decide to plant fruit-trees instead. He will obviously have to remove the flowers to make room for the fruit-trees. In like manner, but on a vaster scale, God, the great gardener, rearranges the universe, according to His design. She does not elaborate upon God's design except to indicate that it is beneficial for man's spiritual development, for the very nature of God is compassion. Because God is compassionate, man can appeal to Him in prayer. It is here where grace comes in. In fact, Ānandamayī Mā speaks of two types of grace. Normally grace operates even within the law of karma. As will be pointed out in detail in connection with the discussion of *sādhanā*, karma operates in a way that even the greatest sinner will eventually "decide" to embark upon the road to liberation. This implies that grace is built into the very mechanism of the universe. It is for this reason that Ānandamayī Mā considers all actions, all experiences beneficial. But in addition to universal grace there is special grace. Through grace, God can wipe out entirely the karmic debts (consequences) of those who appeal to Him sincerely and with utmost devotion. They can be lifted by Him to that transcendent sphere where karma does not operate. While so much of Hindu religious thought is concerned with karma and ways of avoiding rebirth into this valley of tears, the message of Ānandamayī Mā emphasizes the fact that karma and rebirth are nothing but aspects of delusion. Therefore, Ānandamayī Mā discourages people from trying to discover what they might have been in previous incarnations, deeming such inquiry futile, a waste of time: "...when you can visualize five hundred of your former births, you are still limited by number—for there is so very much more than this! ...in Reality there is no question of time and out of time, of day and night, of before and after; so long as you remain enslaved by time there will be birth and death. Actually there is no such thing. It is true that at some stage the memory of previous lives will certainly occur; on the other hand, what is the significance of before and after, since 'I exist throughout eternity.' "

To understand Ānandamayī Mā's views about karma and reincarnation, it is essential to keep in mind that She constantly shifts to and fro between the transcendent and the manifest realm. While She contends that karma has no ultimate reality, She expounds the working of karma on the level of time and space. To illustrate that ordinarily man cannot escape from destiny, i.e., reaping the fruits of his karma, She narrated the following story. The wife and children of a learned Brāhman had been killed by a poisonous snake. Deeply distressed the Brāhman went in pursuit of the snake and finally located it in a nearby forest. As he approached the murderous reptile, it turned into a buffalo. Subsequently the buffalo pounced upon another buffalo and killed him. Immediately thereafter the killer buffalo transformed himself into a beautiful young girl. Two men happened to pass by. Both instantaneously fell in love with the maiden and started to fight with each other over her. When one of them was fatally wounded, the maiden walked off nonchalantly. The Brāhman who had watched the various transformations and the tragic killings finally caught up with the girl and, deeply mystified, asked her who she really was. "I am destiny," she retorted. When he inquired what destiny was in store for him, she informed him that he would die through drowning, whereupon she disappeared. The Brāhman was determined to defy destiny. Since he had lost his family, he had no desire to remain any longer in his home which reminded him of a happiness that no longer existed. He started searching for a new place to settle—a place remote from lakes, rivers or oceans. At long last he came to an apparently ideal location. There he made the acquaintance of a wealthy man who upon hearing about his sad experience invited him to live in his home, to be part of his family. In return he was to become the teacher of the rich man's only son. The son became exceedingly fond of him and when he grew up and got married, he asked his teacher to stay with him and to become the teacher of his future son. In due course a son was born and when he was old enough he received lessons from the Brāhman. One day the family decided to make a pilgrimage to the Ganges, India's most sacred river. Naturally the Brāhman was asked to accompany the family. At first he resisted the family's pleading. When he revealed to them the reason why he was reluctant to participate in the pilgrimage and to bathe in the holy Ganges, they reassured him that they would have a special enclosed bathing area constructed for him and their son. In order not to offend them and especially his beloved pupil, he then agreed to come along. As soon as the Brāhman and the boy entered the enclosed bathing area, the boy changed into a crocodile, seized the Brāhman, broke through the fence and carried him towards the open river. Before drowning him, he addressed the Brāhman: "Don't you recognize me ? I am Destiny."

Another story further reinforces the point that none can resist destiny. An old man had died in a village far from the Ganges. His family who were very devout wanted him to be cremated at the Ganges—the most auspicious site for ending life. The corpse was consequently to be transported to the Ganges by specially hired carriers. Since they were unable to make the trip in one day, the carriers stopped in a village at nightfall and took rest in an inn. It so happened that in that village an extremely pious but poor and lonely old woman was on the point of dying. Her greatest yearning had been to be cremated at the Ganges, but since she had no close relatives it seemed that her desire would go unfulfilled. When she found out about the bier-carriers, it flashed through her mind that this was her chance to attain her goal. Strength surged into her and with utmost determination she managed to remove the corpse from the bier while the carriers were asleep and placed herself on the bier instead. The carriers awoke before dawn and continued the journey in darkness not noticing the change. The moment they reached the Ganges, the old woman died. Upon arrival at the cremation grounds, the carriers discovered that they had carried the wrong corpse. By that time it was too late to correct the "error". The old woman was cremated as she had so ardently hoped for. The other body was found later, already substantially decomposed. Destiny had had its way: "Whatever is due to anyone, anywhere, God will bring it about by a combination of circumstances."

Given Ānandamayī Mā's view concerning destiny, it is not surprising that She urges man to accept all circumstances, all vicissitudes of life as coming from Him. Adverse conditions are not sent to torture us, but to lead us towards total liberation. Probably, of all "adverse" conditions, death is the one which man finds most difficult to accept. It is therefore understandable that devotees frequently come to Ānandamayī Mā when they have suffered the loss of a dear one. A couple who had recently lost their child visited Ānandamayī Mā in Her āśram at Hardwar and wanted to know the significance of premature death. The bliss permeated Mother replied: "Everything happens according to one's karma. It was your karma to serve your son for a few years, and his karma to accept your service. When it was over, God took him away. It is all God's play. Some flowers fall off without bearing fruit..." An American lady told

Ānandamayī Mā that she had lost her husband with whom she had been exceedingly happily married. His death made life meaningless for her. In reply Ānandamayī Mā explained to her that all human attachments eventually have to be given up. God does not want man to have any worldly fetters. When man becomes too engrossed in the world of delusion, the objects of his attachment are withdrawn from him, to remind him of his true home. "Happiness that depends on anything, be it a person, money, comforts, and so forth cannot endure....God alone can give lasting contentment." Ānandamayī Mā also warns Her devotees not to indulge in excessive mourning at the time of bereavement, because this can be an obstacle to the spiritual progress of both the deceased and the survivor. The soul of the deceased is being kept earth-bound by the thoughts of the mourner, while the survivor increases his matter-attachment. He should also remember that the *ātmā* does not die, and that the other person's and his *ātmā* are one. Above all, man should not cry for the loss of a body but rather cry for God. Of course, it is human to shed tears at the death of a loved one but the loss must not paralyze one's vitality: "It is man's duty to remain steady and calm under all circumstances, and to pray only for the welfare of the soul."

Once a male devotee asked Ānandamayī Mā whether by committing suicide upon the death of his beloved wife he would be able to join her. In the strongest possible terms She condemned suicide: "To whom belongs the body that you speak of destroying ? Is this the way a human being talks ? For shame !" And She added that suicide is nothing but a foolish attempt to escape from harvesting one's karma. It only further retards spiritual progress. However, She does not consider that a woman who had become *sati* (literally chaste woman), i.e. a widow who had burnt herself on her husband's funeral pyre, had thereby committed suicide. As far as Ānandamayī Mā was concerned, *sati* was a ritual death, a confirmation of a wife's unconditional loyalty to her husband and an expression of true chastity. "A real *sati* has to be completely steady in mind and body. If entering the fire she suffers, she cannot be called a *sati*." If thus her conduct in life has been totally unblemished, she will be fearless at the time of immolation. In this connection Ānandamayī Mā tells about one of Her ancestors who put one of her fingers into the flame of a candle to test whether she would be able to endure the pain of being burnt. She experienced no pain. Subsequently she ascended her husband's funeral pyre, lay down and remained completely motionless while the flames consumed her body. Westerners will probably be repelled by this story and by Ānandamayī Mā's approval of *sati*. From Her point of view the motive is all-important. The true *sati* is not escaping from life but is fulfilling her duty according to the *dharma* (right way of living) prevailing within her cultural milieu at that time. She is acting selflessly and shows that she is unattached to the delusive body. It must be emphasized that Ānandamayī Mā does not advocate *sati* in this present age.

If we want truly to understand Ānandamayī Mā's attitude towards death, we must constantly remind ourselves that our modern western view of death as man's enemy is alien to Her. "The pilgrim on the path of Immortality never contemplates death. By meditation on the Immortal the fear of death recedes far away; remember this ! In the measure that your contemplation of the One becomes uninterrupted, you will advance towards full, unbroken Realization."

Man's spiritual evolution is greatly affected by the thought he harbours at the time of death: "Just as a leech does not leave its place without hooking on to something else, so the soul at the time of leaving the body hooks on to some kind of new existence according to the state of mind of the dying person." Let no one conclude, however, that he can live according to his whims, indulging in sense pleasures oblivious of God, and that at the moment of death he will be able to catapult himself into the divine presence by thinking the right thoughts. This is a miscalculation, for man is a creature of habit and therefore at death his mind will dwell on those thoughts that have occupied him most during his life.

To substantiate this point Ānandamayī Mā told of a greedy old woman, an oil vendor, who lay upon her death bed. All her life she had sold oil in the bazār. At no time had she granted anyone credit, and never had she given away even the smallest quantity of oil. When beggars asked her for oil, she used to reply: "Not a drop will I give, not a drop." While she was on the verge of dying, her relatives, concerned about her spiritual welfare, tried to make her repeat "Rāma" or "Kṛṣṇa", but all she was capable of uttering was: "Not a drop will I give, not a drop." This had become her mantra.

The foregoing account is meant to show that man's day to day thoughts and activities throughout his life determine his state of consciousness and his spiritual destiny. It is for this reason that Ānandamayī Mā urges Her devotees to be ever concentrated on God, to practise the divine presence, to engage in *sādhanā*. In one sense everyone is practising *sādhanā*, for, as was pointed out in the discussion of grace, all human beings are subject to grace, and all activities ultimately lead towards God. But one should not take too much comfort from this thought, for there are direct roads as well as detours, and some roads are smoother than others. The vast majority of human beings are not consciously travelling anywhere. Nor are they even aware of the fact that they ought to seek God-realization. Completely caught up in delusion, they focus all their attention on the material world. But the world is so constituted that it cannot provide lasting contentment. Because man has within him a drive for perfection, he is bound to be frustrated in an imperfect world. Man is attracted to material pleasures initially because they are tangible. His essential nature, however, is spirit and spirit cannot be satisfied with material food. The starvation of the spirit is not noticeable at first. Only when material objects have disappointed him, does he begin consciously to seek in a non-material direction and thus begins deliberately his *sādhanā*. The great stimulant to spiritual endeavour is pain and suffering, man's true friends, according to Ānandamayī Mā: "Remember, one is born to experience various kinds of joys and sorrows according to one's desire. For the time being, God comes to you in the disguise of suffering. He is purifying you in this manner..The suffering is for your own best. A mother gives a slap to her beloved child for its own good, in order to keep it on the right path. When a fond mother gives her baby a bath, the child may scream desperately, yet the mother will not let the baby go until she has thoroughly washed and scrubbed him.." Thus suffering is a necessity, a means of purification, and a means of instilling ardour into man to seek God, the only source of happiness. If man only knew that God is most relishable. But just as someone who has never eaten a *rasagulla* (Bengali sweet), cannot imagine its sweetness, man who has not experienced the divine, cannot know the supreme bliss of God's presence.

To become aware of God's presence and ultimately become one with Him, one has to engage in *sādhanā*. This requires effort at first, but success is not attained until *sādhanā* has become effortless. The beginner on the path will have to exert himself, use all his will-power to overcome the pull of the world. Ānandamayī Mā likens *sādhanā* to a bitter pill prescribed by the doctor for our cure. Similarly, spiritual effort appears unpleasant initially. Gross pleasures of the senses are easily accessible, the more subtle joys of the spirit can only be attained after a complete redirection of our energies, a re-focussing of our attention and a conquest of habits established over many lives. Yet there is no alternative, the bitter pill of *sādhanā* has to be swallowed, if one wants to be healed from suffering. When steady effort has resulted in the first glimpses of God's bliss, one's enthusiasm becomes aroused. Worldly attractions decrease as God's magnetic pull is being felt, and in the end we approach effortlessly the divine goal: "To realize God means to realize one's Self. How can there be strain while engaging in the essential thing for oneself ?" As we identify with our true Self, delusive selfishness drops off. We find freedom in God. Unfortunately, many of us delay swallowing the medicine. When old age comes we lament; "Eventide has come and life is ebbing away. O Lord, have mercy upon me and take me across." But rarely can we at that stage muster that amount of energy required to attract the divine grace.

In general, one's desire for God is the most important element for a successful *sādhanā*. We must crave for God "with all our heart, all our mind, and all our soul." We must yearn for God as the shipwrecked sailor longs for the shore. We must be as intent in our search for God as the businessman is upon financial success. All other duties must be subordinated to *sādhanā*.

"Infinite are the *sādhanās*.." There are no hard and fast rules. The path most suitable for one person may in no way be ideal for someone else. Mātājī places special importance on repetition of the divine name, "keeping one's mouth sweet," as She sometimes calls it.* The bliss permeated Mother also urges Her devotees to listen to religious talks by mahātmās, to study sacred writings, to engage in *kīrtana*, always keeping in mind that all techniques are meant to acquaint man with God until such time that God becomes an ever-present reality, that He, the One is perceived behind all manifestations. Whether one calls Him Rāma, Kṛṣṇa, Christ or Buddha is immaterial. Once while Ānandamayī Mā was walking through a village, the local inhabitants asked Her which name of God they ought to invoke. Ānandamayī Mā raised three fingers of Her right hand and, pointing to each of them said: "This is Rāma, this Kṛṣṇa, this Śiva. Now catch hold of one !" As far as Haṭha Yoga is concerned, Ānandamayī Mā points out that normally its only goal is physical agility, which by itself is of little value. If one practises it, however, to attain stillness of the body, in order to perceive the divine better, then Haṭha Yoga is beneficial.

When asked whether formal worship (*pūjā*) is necessary for the attainment of Self-realization, Ānandamayī Mā often emphasizes the fact that ritual rightly applied is often of great help when one practises *sādhanā*. Through regular worship one cultivates devotion, one establishes an intimate relationship with Him whom one worships. Loving devotion will lead to a tangible experience of the divine presence. There will subsequently come a time, provided one continues ardently one's daily *pūjā*, when He is seen in all objects, and then He alone exists. Is there then any need to worship, if worshipper and the object of worship are One ? There is no longer a necessity for worship. Still one may continue to do *pūjā* in the knowledge that the One who is beyond manifestation is also immanent in his creation and thus also in *pūjā*.

As can be expected, Ānandamayī Mā deals at length with the role of a guru in relation to *sādhanā*. While Hinduism, on the whole, attaches great importance to the role of a guru, She considers it possible to engage in *sādhanā* without the bodily presence of a guru. In one way, She argues, everyone has a

* One not too perceptive devotee had taken Her advice literally and had eaten sugarcandy daily. After a year's "practice" he complained that he had not yet attained God-realization !

guru, since only One exists and the One manifesting through various people, objects, circumstances, teaches us, even though we may not be aware of it. Also, the quest for an outer guru will eventually lead to the discovery of the inner guru, one's true Self. She warns, however, that it is easy to mistake the prompting of one's mind for the inner guru. Only the one who is "free from anger, greed, delusion, pride, egotism" is attuned to the inner guru. Normally She advises devotees to look for an "outer" guru: "Go and sit under a tree..." The tree signifies a saint, a truly enlightened person who can lead one to God. "Saints may be compared to trees: they always point upwards and grant shade and shelter to all. They are free from likes and dislikes and whoever seeks refuge in them wholeheartedly, will find peace." She adds: "Just as water cleanses everything by its mere contact, even so the sight, touch, blessing nay the very remembrance of a real sādhu, little by little, clears away all impure desires and longings." Finding a genuine guru is indeed a blessing. One must follow his advice unconditionally. While obeying the guru and treating him with reverence, one must not become attached to his personality. The true guru will naturally emphasize the fact that he is a mere vehicle of God and discourage personal veneration. It is the false guru—still in ego-consciousness—who permits the development of a personality cult. What if one unwittingly has found a false guru ? Even this is only a seeming misfortune, for there will come a time when one awakens from one's error and then one will assuredly know how to discover a genuine guru. There is another aspect to be considered. More important than the guru is the devotee's own attitude, because in the ultimate sense, no one else can give us Self-realization. We have to find it. Thus it is conceivable that a sincere seeker, seeing God behind his guru, however imperfect that guru might be, will be able to go beyond the guru and reach God.

In one's *sādhanā* the guru's help normally is particularly important for learning the art of concentration on God, i.e., meditation. The restless mind, flitting from one aspect of this world of multiplicity to another, must be brought under control so that the many are eliminated and the One perceived. Numerous are the methods that gurus suggest to their disciples. Ānandamayī Ma tells the story of a guru who noticed that his disciple was making no progress in meditation. Thereupon the guru asked the disciple whether there was anyone or anything that interested him intensely. Without hesitation the disciple said that his main interest was his buffalo. "Then go to your meditation room and concentrate on the buffalo. Visualize him and do not let your mind wander from thinking about the buffalo." The following day the guru knocked at the door of the meditation room and asked the disciple to come out. There followed a period of silence. Then the disciple replied in an exceedingly deep voice that it was impossible for him to leave his room, because his horns could not pass through the door. He obviously had achieved a high degree of concentration! The moral of the story is that deep concentration leads to identification, to merger. Actually, all human beings are potential yogis, able to concentrate on what interests them. For hours men can sit and play cards, watch movies or shows, or bend all their efforts to amassing money or passing examinations. All that is needed, is a shift of emphasis from the worldly to God.

In agreement with the mystics of all ages in the east or in the west, Ānandamayī Mā points out that one of the greatest obstacles on the path back to God is our ego. "Always bear this in mind: Everything is in God's hands, and you are His tool to be used by Him as He pleases. Try to grasp the significance of 'all is His', and you will immediately feel free from all burdens. What will be the result of your surrender to Him? None will seem alien, all will be your very own, your Self." The idea "I am apart, separate from everything else" must go. Man has to learn to empty himself completely of desire, pride, passion and any awareness of "I am" or "I do." So long as we have not attained total emptiness, God, who is everything cannot occupy us, cannot pour his infinite divine bliss into us. Ānandamayī Mā's view on emptiness is similar to the Zen concept of emptiness and the concept of the most intimate poverty (*eigentlichste Armut*) of Meister Eckhart who says: "...if God wants to act in the soul, He Himself must be the place in which He acts..."

Our discussion of *sādhanā* has been entirely concerned with spiritual matters so far. Does service to humanity have no part in one's *sādhanā*? This question obviously will occur to westerners among whom religion has at present almost become identified with social service. They are likely to ask whether Ānandamayī Mā is totally unconcerned about human welfare. Does She ignore the enormous physical suffering of the masses which is a most conspicuous and depressing element of Indian life ? Melita Maschmann, the German novelist, in a way, addressed herself to this question. During her stay in Calcutta she met Mother Theresa, the Catholic nun who has dedicated her life to the founding of orphanages, medical centers, homes for the aged, in other words, has been engaged in social welfare work. Miss Maschmann was deeply impressed by the inspiring dedication of Mother Theresa to alleviating the plight of the unfortunates. She mentioned to one of Ānandamayī Mā's disciples that it seemed to her that, in contradistinction to Ānandamayī Mā, the Catholic nun was truly living up to the commandment that one should love one's neighbour as oneself. The immediate reply of the disciple was that service to mankind was precisely what Ānandamayī Mā was doing all the time. Ānandamayī Mā would probably say that each one has to play a different role in God's cosmic drama. One role has been assigned to Mother Theresa, another to Ānandamayī Mā. Actually, She does stress the importance of helping others not only spiritually: "Widening your shrivelled heart, make the interests of others your own and serve them as much as you can by sympathy, kindness, presents and so forth. So long as one enjoys the things of this world and has needs and wants, it is necessary to minister to the needs of one's fellowmen. Otherwise one cannot be called a human being. Whenever you have the opportunity, give to the poor, feed the hungry, nurse the sick...do service as a religious duty and you will come to know by direct perception that the person served, the one who serves and the act of service are separate only in appearance."

While it is obvious that Ānandamayī Mā agrees that alleviating physical suffering if carried out in a self-less spirit, contributes to one's spiritual advance, She herself, just as the Buddha, is concerned with getting at the root of all suffering, to eliminate it once and for all. Her diagnosis is that alienation from the One (one's true Self) is the basic cause of all suffering. Therefore by doing away with physical suffering one deals with the symptoms, not with the underlying cause of the disease. In fact, onesided concentration on eliminating physical suffering may even prolong the disease. Here we must keep in mind that Ānandamayī Mā's whole teaching emphasizes the fact that all seemingly negative experiences ultimately have positive consequences. As has been stated earlier, suffering is really a means for ending suffering: "Just as fire burns away all dross and rubbish, so the three-fold suffering purges man's heart from all impurity and results in a growing single-mindedness in his search after Truth. When he becomes deeply conscious of his weakness and tormented by the thought of his undesirable impulses and distressing characteristics, when afflictions like poverty, bereavement or humiliation make him feel his life is futile, then and then only does he develop real faith and religious fervour, and becomes anxious to surrender himself at the feet of the Supreme Being. Suffering should therefore be welcomed. Never does the soft moonlight appear more soothing than after the scorching heat of a summer day." The great promise is: "By sorrow does the Lord dispel sorrow and by adversity does He destroy adversity. When this is done He sends no more suffering—this must be borne in mind at all times."

Ānandamayī Mā's views on suffering and poverty are so diametrically opposed to the whole philosophy of modern western man that it would require revolutionary changes in his attitude for him to agree with Her. All our attempts to wipe out poverty and the doctors' frantic quest for eliminating physical pain are undertaken in the belief that perfection can be attained by physical means. They are based on a dualistic view of the universe which labels certain things as evil without acknowledging their redeeming potential. Above all, this applies to modern western man's aversion to suffering which is regarded as an unmitigated evil. In contrast, Ānandamayī Mā holds up to us the attitude towards pain as exemplified in India's great epic, the *Rāmāyaṇa.* There, Hanumān, the loyal devotee of Rāma (an *avatāra* of Viṣṇu), built a bridge to Laṅkā (Ceylon), in order to rescue Sītā, Rāma's consort, who had been abducted to Laṅkā by the demon King Rāvaṇa. During the construction of the bridge, Hanumān accidentally hurt a squirrel. The squirrel thereupon complained to Rāma and demanded that in punishment Rāma step upon Hanumān. Rāma did so and told Hanumān not to commit such a deed again, if he did not want to suffer similar punishment. But Hanumān retorted: "I will very often commit such faults so that I may repeatedly feel the pressure of your feet."

Further to stress the purifying effect of suffering, Ānandamayī Mā tells the story of a pitcher which became a *pūjā* vessel. Originally it had been just an ordinary clump of earth on which people trampled and into which people dug with sharp spades. Later the earth was taken to a potter who kneaded it and put it on a potter's wheel, turned it around, moulded it and fired it to make it hard and solid. Only then it was fit to be used as a pūjā vessel and sacred Ganges water poured into it. Similarly human vessels have to be moulded to become fit instruments for the divine spirit. "Be enduring as earth...Divine Life will be awakened in you." By looking at suffering from a truly monistic point of view, another dimension emerges: "Who is it that loves and who that suffers ? He alone stages a play with Himself.. The individual suffers because he perceives duality... Find the One everywhere and in everything and there will be an end to pain and suffering."

With Ānandamayī Mā's stress on finding the One as the cure-all, what is the role of renunciation ? Is total renunciation required of those who are earnest about their *sādhanā* ? Actually the mass of mankind are renunciants of a sort, for they renounce God, who is Supreme Bliss, for the sake of paltry temporary material pleasures. When that true Reality has been contacted, all cravings will drop off. "Worldly things seem tedious, quite foreign to oneself; worldly talk loses all its appeal, becomes devoid of interest and at a further stage even painful..To the extent that one becomes estranged from the world of the senses one draws nearer to God." If man only knew that he is settling for synthetic pleasures while he could have real ever-lasting joy, the question of renunciation would not be a matter of struggle. As it is, only few are ready to pledge themselves formally to complete renunciation and become homeless wanderers, (*saṁnyāsis*). Ānandamayī Mā warns strongly against taking the vows of renunciation before one is truly prepared for this step. As long as one is inwardly plagued by cravings and prone to hatred, anger and fear, withdrawing to the Himalayas is delusion. Mere outward renunciation will not do. Wearing the ochre robe of renunciation may help some to live up to their vows, but eventually one must reach a state where one is no longer in need of such a reminder. After all, even an ochre robe is part of delusion. It might also tempt one to spiritual pride. No fast and hard rules apply to any path. To illustrate this point She mentioned that She had met a man who had been a *saṁnyāsi*. After years of strenuous effort he had made no apparent spiritual progress and in desperation he had abandoned his life of renunciation.. Shortly thereafter he attained enlightenment.

If one cannot vow oneself to total renunciation, one can use the life of a householder for spiritual advance. Untold opportunities arise in one's householder existence to practise *sādhanā*. One can serve God in the form of one's wife and children. One's home can become an āśram in which the whole family jointly worships. After a few children are born, husband and wife ought to live like brother and sister, forgoing sexual relations. In general, Ānandamayī Mā urges householders to pattern their lives upon those of the ancient *ṛṣis* (seers, sages). Accordingly, when one approaches the age of fifty-five or sixty, one should withdraw from worldly activities. One has played one's part, fulfilled one's social duties. Wisdom demands that the remaining few years will be spent for God alone. How different this is from modern western man's desperate attempts to prolong youth so that he can continue to indulge in sense pleasures, to avoid facing his Self ! How much time and money he expends to hide signs of ageing ! How great is his skill in devising new forms of entertainment to divert his attention from the thought of death ! Ānandamayī Mā goes so far as to sanction withdrawing from family life at an earlier age, if one is consumed by the fire of renunciation. But by no means does She approve of withdrawal from marital obligations for those whose motive it is to evade family responsibilities. One's yearning for renunciation must be as intense as that of the Buddha who left his family to discover the cause of suffering. Significantly, the present Indian constitution has a provision granting divorce in cases where one marriage partner wishes to renounce the world. It is most unlikely that need for such legislation will occur in the United States.

By advocating a return to the life of the *ṛṣis*, Ānandamayī Mā clearly indicates Her preference for the value system of ancient India. In 1961, the then Governor of Maharashtra, Śrī Śrī

Prakāśa, asked Her what cure She envisioned for the moral and spiritual decay of modern society. In reply She pleaded for a return to the ancient Vedic system whose foundation was *brahmacarya,* i.e., young men and women lived a celibate life and received spiritual training from their guru before embarking upon the householder path.* She considers the *brahmacarya* stage essential for a stable society. Only if young people are taught self-control, even-mindedness, unselfishness and God-centeredness, would they be well-grounded in the art of living. Then *brahmacarya* would automatically lead to *brahmavidyā* (knowledge of Brahman, God). Traditional is also Ānandamayī Mā's attitude towards the selection of marriage partners. In view of the fact that young people are likely to base their choice of a marriage partner on physical attraction primarily, it is preferable that their parents make the choice. She takes it for granted that parents will have a more mature judgment than their offsprings and that they will give primary consideration to the welfare of their sons and daughters. This is indeed a noble ideal, but in practice many parents fail to live up to Her lofty standards. Bride and bridegroom should not see each other before the wedding. She compares such an act to offering for *pūjā* a fruit that has been pecked at by a bird.

With Her strong emphasis on the sacredness of marital ties, it is not surprising that Ānandamayī Mā counsels: "There is only one marriage." Consequently She never advises a second marriage even for widows. It should be pointed out, however, that She in no way discriminates against those who come to Her who have already been married twice or even three times.

Her attitude towards the role of women is both traditional and modern. She does emphasize woman's duty to be loyal and obedient to Her husband. At the same time She envisages a revolutionary change in the status of women: "It marks the spirit of the present time that women will take their place at the helm of society and men ply the oars." The spiritual training of women must not in any way be inferior to that of men. "Then you will see how the lives of both men and women will be ennobled and raised to a higher level...a renaissance of Hindu

* Only in the early Vedic Age (1500-800 B.C.) do women seem to have received a formal religious education.

society will follow." Does Ānandamayī Mā possibly conceive Her own role as a spiritual leader characteristic of the new age ? She has in fact taken several concrete steps to demonstrate the changed status of women. Not only did She perform the sacred thread ceremony—a monopoly of men for many hundred years—upon Herself, but in 1940 also arranged for it to be performed upon three of Her women devotees. Consequently all three of them recite regularly the *gāyatrī mantra* (specially sacred verse usually recited by men only).* In 1965 a *Nārāyaṇa Śilā* (blackish stone, a symbol of Lord Nārāyaṇa) was brought to Ānandamayī Mā. The bliss permeated Mother thereupon instructed a woman renunciant, Brahmacāriṇī Udās, to perform regular *pūjā* of the *Nārāyaṇa Śilā.* Again, this was contrary to tradition. When upon the death of Her husband, Her mother, Didimā, decided to take the vow of renunciation, a distinguished guru, Swāmī Mangal Giri, was approached. At first he declined to accept Didimā as a complete renunciant. Obviously through the intercession of Ānandamayī Mā he relented. Didimā became Swāmī Muktānanda Giri. This too was most uncommon, for the title swāmī is rarely conferred upon a woman.

It is necessary not to misconstrue Ānandamayī Mā's innovative gestures. In no way can they be seen as woman's liberationist moves in the western sense. The emphasis is on spiritual equality. Above all, the goal is liberation from sense enslavement and egocentricity. This is contrary to the contemporary western movement which chiefly claims the right for women to indulge in sense and pursue egotistic goals on par with men.

Ānandamayī Mā also holds traditional views towards food. She considers it important to eat *sāttvic* (pure) foods, i.e. no meat, fish, eggs, garlic or onions. She does, however, broaden the concept of food to mean anything taken in by one's mind or senses. Man, therefore, should abstain from impure thoughts and feelings, such as lust, greed, hatred. envy and anger. Naturally, pure thoughts take precedence over pure food. And yet repeatedly Ānandamayī Mā makes it clear that it is unwise to belittle ritual, to think that one may easily do away with the

* Four other brahmacāriṇīs have been given sacred threads in recent years.

externals. There is a subtle interrelationship between internal and external worship. It is on those grounds that She upholds traditional religious ceremonies including *yajñas* (fire sacrifices). From 1947 to 1950 a giant fire sacrifice was performed at Her āśram in Vārāṇasi, with the participation of holy men from all over India.

Her respect for tradition even extends to the institution of caste which, for a westerner, is most difficult to understand. At a time when many intellectuals in India condemn the caste system and the Indian constitution has in theory at least outlawed it, caste restrictions are enforced in the āśrams of Ānandamayī Mā. The bliss permeated Mother Herself is beyond caste. Just as did India's greatest philosopher, Śaṅkarācārya, She can say: "No birth, no death, no caste have I." All human beings are equal in Her eyes. But the majority of those who surround Her are strictly orthodox and concerned about contamination. Foreigners who seek *darśana* from Ānandamayī Mā discover that they are treated as casteless. They must eat and sleep separately and avoid coming close to the kitchen, for their very presence in the kitchen would contaminate the food. These rules apply even to Brahmacāriṇī Ātmānanda. Melita Maschmann in particular was disturbed about this seemingly inconsistent attitude of Ānandamayī Mā. After all, if only One exists, why stress caste distinctions ? In a talk with Ānandamayī Mā she aired her feelings. The Mother then explained that during Her *sādhanā* She had behaved in a most unconventional manner and therefore alienated many orthodox Hindus. Once She had consulted a *mahātmā* who had advised Her to abide by Hindu traditions, otherwise She would keep away the orthodox element of the population. While She Herself continued to treat everyone alike irrespective of caste background, She decided not to interfere with the enforcement of caste rules. She was fully aware of the fact that foreigners incurred some hardships thereby, but since there were only a handful of foreigners involved, She did not deem it right to make it impossible for orthodox Hindus to enjoy Her presence. The majority of Her followers were still living on a level of consciousness where abidance by caste restrictions was important for them. At the right time they would transcend caste feeling, but one could not artificially accelerate this development. She seems convinced that the time for abolishing the caste system has not arrived. Such an attitude must be totally incomprehensible to western activists engaged in social crusades.

Western Faustian man whose dynamism is fed by the notion of progress will not be enamoured by Ānandamayī Mā's view of progress. Once during a trip to Baidyanāth Dhām in 1938 Ānandamayī Mā was shown newly built houses which starkly contrasted with some old dilapidated buildings in the background. But Ānandamayī Mā was not impressed. She pointed out to Didi that there had been a time when the old houses had been brand new. Rise and decay was the eternal *leitmotif* in the realm of matter. Was it then futile to try to make improvements ? She sees nothing wrong in technical advance, provided it is used for spiritual ends. After all, She Herself now uses trains and motor cars to travel to various places. When Her beloved devotee Dr. Gopīnāth Kavirāj was very ill, She saw to it that he was placed in a modern hospital with the most up-to-date equipment. It is technical progress for mere progress' sake that She rejects. Basing one's philosophy on material progress alone is like building a house on a foundation of sand. The ultimate criterion for deciding any problem must be: "Will this action lead me towards God-realization or not?" This is the kind of pragmatism which is wholly alien to materialists. Ānandamayī Mā could ask the hardheaded western realists whether technological progress had done away with greed, hatred, fear. Has it supplied man with peace and bliss ? If worshippers of technology would ask Her whether She is not at least impressed by man's ability to land on the moon and to make possible travels to far distant planets in the near future, She would in all likelihood counter: "This is indeed a part of the infinite manifestation of the divine *līlā*. But what of it ? Will reaching Mars or Jupiter diminish to any extent man's selfishness, fears and hatreds ? The truly ascetic discipline and determination of the astronauts, if used for the purpose of *sādhanā*, would assuredly lead to quick results. Finding the One, one makes contact with Him who is the origin and power behind all planets. In His presence all human pettiness dissolves into nothing. Why not then try for the 'Grand Prix of Self-realization? "This alone is worthy of a human being." In view of the fact that more and more westerners begin to have second thoughts about technological progress, the views of Ānandamayī Mā may have more relevance for us than we may at first admit. To those who seek perfection She suggests self-perfection; to those in search of a revolution, self-revolution; and to those suffering from alienation she offers oneness with the very source of their being. "Only actions that kindle man's divine nature are worthy of the name of action...Man's calling is to aspire to the realization of Truth, to tread the excellent path that leads to Immortality."

At the Congress of Indian Philosophy held in Dacca in 1929 someone asked Ānandamayī Mā: "If the human character and everybody becomes unselfish, will the world then become perfect ?" Her answer was: "But such it is already." She sees a harmony that escapes us who are still enmeshed in delusion, mesmerized by the world's apparent duality. She is exuding bliss because She is in constant contact with that One whom the Hindus define as *Sat Cit Ānanda* (ever existent, ever conscious bliss). But that bliss of Hers is of little use to us unless we too experience it. Therefore She urges us: "Become drinkers of nectar, all of you—drinkers of the wine of immortality. Tread the path of immortality, where no death exists and no disease."

APPENDIX I

Selected Sayings of **Anandamayi Ma**

Accepting all conditions of life—whatever they be—as His gift abide in fortitude and do service.

Endeavour to keep your thought centered at all times on the divine Name or Form that appeals to you most. Let your mind be turned exclusively towards God—then, and then only, may you hope for peace.

Man must behave as a hero. During spells of misfortune he must abide in fortitude and patience. Time never stands still.

To live upto the highest ideals seems irksome at first, but ultimately brings real well-being and peace.

The word *manuṣ** (man) itself gives the clue to what man should really be; a being who is self-aware. Even if he has slipped and fallen, is it not his bounden duty to use as a lever the very earth to which he has tumbled and raise himself up again ? ...As a man constant effort is his duty. If he does not awaken to the consciousness of his own Self, what has he achieved ? He has but wasted his life. How many lives are frittered away, age after age in endless coming and going. Find out who you are ! Discover the significance of the round of births and deaths, its cause and where it leads ! When man becomes a traveller on the path to his inner Being the distance that separates him from his Goal gradually vanishes. You will most certainly have to undertake this pilgrimage to Immortality, trampling under foot hundreds and hundreds of obstacles and impediments. This is the kind of manliness that has to be awakened...

It is the will of the Almighty that prevails. By living in harmony with this will and becoming an instrument in His Hands you should try to realize Him.

The lute of man's short life is strung with so many strings; they have to be cut asunder. There is no real substance to these many strings. It is futile to let one's thoughts be occupied with

* *man* means mind and *huṣ* consciousness.

the ties by which one is bound. Why behave like a fool and return again and again to this world of illusion ?

Many feel the urge to create a new and better world. Rather than let your thoughts dwell on such matters, you should concentrate on that by the contemplation of which there is hope of perfect peace.

A person who does not for the love of God and with a cheerful heart discharge himself of whatever responsibility that may fall to his lot at any time, will find life excessively burdensome and never be able to accomplish anything. Man should joyfully serve the world with the conviction that all service is His service. Work done in such a spirit helps to purify the mind and heart.

Why speak of Self-realization in the future ? It *is* here and now —only the veil that hides it has to be destroyed. What is meant by 'destroyed' ? That which in any case is doomed to destruction is to be destroyed. When the veil falls to pieces THAT which eternally IS shines forth—the ONE, Self-luminous.

It is by crying and pining for Him that the One is found. In times of adversity and distress as well as in times of well-being and good fortune try to seek refuge in the One alone. Keep in mind that whatever He, the All-beneficent, the Fountain of Goodness, does, is wholly for the best.

Worldly life is indeed a battle-field. By becoming conscious of one's spiritual wealth one must strive to emerge victorious from the battle. A person who knows that he is ignorant must be credited with having most certainly attained to some measure of knowledge.

He alone knows to whom He will reveal Himself under which form. By what path and in what manner He attracts any particular man to Himself with great force is incomprehensible to the human intelligence. The Path differs indeed for different pilgrims. Very often He destroys misfortune by misfortune and annihilates sorrow by sorrow.

The love of God alone is desirable for a human being. He who has brought you forth, He who is your Father, Mother, Friend, Beloved and Lord, who has given you everything, has nourished you with the ambrosia streaming from His own being—by whatever name you invoke Him—that name you should bear in mind at all times.

The Supreme Power Itself is directly present in all forms under which It is worshipped. Cry out to It and to It alone. The Supreme Power cannot remain indifferent to the inconsolable weeping of Its offspring. Thus it is the One who deals severe blows—yet again Himself consoles by His loving embrace.

Man appears to be the embodiment of want. Want is what he thinks about and want indeed is what he obtains. Contemplate your true being—or else there will be want, wrong action, helplessness, distress and death.

"There" also one obtains a pension. The pension you earn in this world lasts only as long as you live, while that pension never ends. By what grace of His such a pension is granted is impossible to tell. If anything is to be desired at all, one should desire this Grace.

Apart from seeking refuge in the contemplation of God, there is no way of becoming liberated from worldly anxiety and annoyance. Engage in whatever practice that helps to keep the mind centered in Him who is manifest as Creation, Preservation, and Dissolution. To regret one's bad luck only troubles the mind and ruins the body; it has no other effect—keep this in mind ! He by whose law everything has been wrought, He alone should be remembered.

How can there be an ego where the Ātmā is ? In the sphere of "mine and yours," there the ego exists, does it not ? Renunciation and attraction dwell side by side. He Himself is both change and immutability. Live for the revelation of the Self hidden within you. He who does not live thus is committing suicide. Try to remove the veil of ignorance by the contemplation of God. Endeavour to tread the path of Immortality: become a follower of the Immortal.

In the field of His play even getting means losing. This is but the nature of its movement. Think of Him Who cannot be lost. Meditate on Him alone, on Him, the Fountatin of Goodness. Pray to Him; depend on Him. Try to give more time to *japa* and meditation. Surrender your mind at His Feet. Endeavour to sustain *japa* and meditation without a break.

It is necessary to try and dedicate to the Supreme every single action of one's daily life. From the moment one wakes in the morning until one falls asleep at night one should endeavour to sustain this attitude of mind. By so doing one will gradually come to feel: How can I offer Him greed, anger and other undesirable qualities of this kind ? To Him who is so infinitely dear to me—who is my very own ? Does one give that which is bad to one's nearest and dearest ? As one continues to reflect in this way one finally becomes incapable of doing anything bad or undesirable. Then, when at His Lotus-feet one has sacrificed without reserve whatever small power one possesses, so that there is nothing left that one may call one's own, do you know what He does at that fortunate moment ? Out of your littleness He makes you perfect, whole, and then nothing remains to be desired or achieved. The moment your self-dedication becomes complete, at that very instant occurs the revelation of the indivisible, unbroken Perfection which is ever revealed by the Self.

APPENDIX II

Advice for Daily Living by **Anandamayi Ma**

This daughter of yours implores you all to do one thing, my good fathers and mothers. You are anxious to obtain relief from all the ills you are burdened with. You know when a person is ill he requires both right diet and medicine: your medicine is the repetition of the Divine Name and contemplation of its meaning; your daily diet will be self-control. Practise these two together on one special day in the week, or in a fortnight or at least on one day in the month. The more you can, the better. You should observe the following rules during that special day of devotion:

I. OBSERVE truth in speech, thought and action.

II. EXTREME simplicity in food and dress.

III. KEEP the mind serene for that day preferring the eternal to the temporal; with keen devotion dwell constantly on His forms, His messages to man and His glories as revealed in the *Gītā*.

IV. TRY during that day always to bear in mind that God sends all the worries of life for edifying yourself.

V. KEEP up a spirit of service for that day believing that your parents, teachers, children, wives, neighbours, are all so many channels through whom your services to them always reach Him.

VI. EVER strengthen the conviction that you are dwelling in Truth, growing in the bosom of the Good and losing yourself to find Him more and more from day to day.

VII. EVER remember that the joys and sorrows of the world are fleeting shadows of your own self; playing with the divine forces brings in everlasting peace and happiness.

VIII. GIVE your mind a long rope to play with Him: rejoice in the beauties of His forms, attributes, and graces, and in what is stated about Him in the *śāstras* (sacred writings) or what has been said about Him by the saints of all lands.

IX. When you feel you are not progressing spiritually, always think that you alone are responsible for the setback; fortify your will with more and more strength, with a purer or higher ego-sense, i.e., 'I must call out His name', I will worship Him,' 'I must learn to love Him.' This I-ness pointing to God is better than the self-ego.

X. Remember always during the whole day, repetition of His name has enough power to wash away all sins if there be any, whether of this life or of the past ones.

APPENDIX III

The *Cakras* As Seen and Interpreted by **Anandamayi Ma**

Bhāijī in *Mother as Revealed to Me* relates that once when he visited Ānandamayī Mā in Shah-bagh, he noticed that She had drawn some figures on the floor. When he inquired about the significance of the figures, She told him that they were representations of the *cakras* as She had observed them. Before giving Her description, a few preliminary remarks are needed. According to tantric* teachings there are seven *cakras* along the spinal column. The spinal column itself contains two nerve currents *iḍā* and *piṅgalā*. In the center of the spinal column is a passage called *suṣumnā*. The life energy (*prāṇa*) is normally coiled up at the base of the spine and therefore referred to as *kuṇḍalinī* (that which is coiled up, serpent power). Through austerities and a special yogic technique *prāṇāyāma* (life force control), the *kuṇḍalinī* is released and thereupon moves upward along the spinal centres until it reaches the seventh center, *sahasrāra* (thousand petalled lotus). At that moment enlightenment has been attained. The forms and colours of the various *cakras* as well as the whole process of liberating the *kuṇḍalini* have been brought to the attention of westerners by Arthur Avalon (Sir John George Woodroffe) in his book *Serpent Power*.

"While walking about at noon, I sat down here in a yogic posture, when I observed some lotus-like vital centers from the highest centre in the brain right down along the spinal cord to its lowest end, a few inches apart from one another. I saw clearly that from the lowest tip of the spinal cord upwards there lay many finer and finer centres, of which only the six chief-ones have been drawn here. I have not drawn them deliberately, my hand has of itself moved about on the floor and this is how these pictures have come about. You should note that through these vital areas of interlacing nerves function the inherited impulses, acquired dispositions, emotions, various urges, thought-cycles, and notions of life and death, etc. which find

* Special, at times unorthodox, rituals found in Hinduism and Buddhism.

their way downwards from the highest brain-center, in response to stimulation from all the sense organs. Streams of life and of vital fluid course swiftly or slowly through those channels and guide the life-processes and thought-currents of man. Just as you find that earth, water, fire, air and the space beyond the atmosphere, interpenetrate one another, so also these six chief centers lie inside the body apparently one above the other, but functioning in mutual interdependence as one vital chain. A little reflection will convince you that the play of life goes on in the upper centers of your body when your thoughts are pure and full of bliss. Just as you find that springs of water lying at the bottom of a well or a tank keep up a constant supply, or just as the sap of plant-life is underground deep down about the roots, so at the lowest end of the spinal cord (mūlādhara) lies asleep the fountain of the giant vital forces derived ultimately from the sun, from where issue forth the streams of your life. When with great patience and sanctity you strive to purify your inner and outer vehicles, the resulting vibrations of your thoughts strike ever higher and higher centers, releasing their tension, freeing the pent up life-force at the lowest center to seek outlets upwards. Then all the lethargy, primal urges and *saṁskāras** of the devotee gradually fade away like mists before the sun's rays; along with the unleashing of the block, our attachment to the objects of the senses begins to relax, and the inner life starts taking shape.

When the upward drive of the life-force reaches the vital center at the parting of the eyebrows, the inner stream of the vital fluid flows with ease and purity quite evenly all over the human system, with the result that the devotee comes to realize something of the nature of the ego, the world and creation. If a man continues in this stage for long, all his prenatal, inherited dispositions and urges gradually become weaker and weaker; his mind reaches ever higher and higher levels of contemplation, ever deeper centers of the life-force.

When the devotee reaches beyond the highest vital center which is situated between the eyebrows, (*dvidala cakra*), his mental powers merge in the supra-mental, his ego dissolves in *Mahābhāva* (highest ecstasy, supreme love for God) and he finds his eternal

* mental dispositions, often brought over from previous lives.

refuge in *Svarūpa* (His own true Self). He then goes into *samādhi*, a state of perpetual bliss.

As the various vital centers begin to open up, different sounds are perceived inwardly and the devotee comes to feel the sounds of conches, bells, flutes, etc. all merging in the cosmic rhythm of one great voice of infinite silence. At that stage no thought or object of the outside world can distract his attention. As he advances, his being gets dissolved in the bottomless depth of that blissful music that pervades the whole universe, and he finds eternal repose."

When Bhāijī showed Her the *cakras* as depicted in Sir John George Woodroffe's *Serpent Power*, She retorted: "I have not read about these centers in any book, nor have I ever before heard anything about them from anyone. The description I gave is from my actual experience. And She added: "The colours of those vital centers that you find in the pictures are but their external tinge. The same substance of which our brain is made also forms these plexuses, but their shapes, structures and functions vary. Each one has its special characteristics and distinctive qualities like the eye, or the ear, or the navel or even the lines on the palms of your hands. In them there is everchanging play of various colours and sounds and their symbols called *seed mantras*, all being natural results of the movement of the life-force and the flow of the vital fluid. During the earlier stages, when various *mantras* issued from these lips accompanied by transformations of the breath, at times questions like 'What are these ?' flashed across my mind. The reply came from within and the inner structure of all those plexuses became distinctly visible like the pictures you have put before me. When a person regularly prays, performs *pūjās* and yogic practices, meditates and reflects on the higher truths of existence with sufficient concentration, the mind substance gets purified, thoughts become refined and the centers unfold themselves. Otherwise no human being can find an escape from the storm of physical urges like lust, greed and anger."

APPENDIX IV

Selected poems dedicated to **Anandamayi Ma**
by some of Her devotees

The Song of a Crazy Fellow
Song by Bhāijī
(translated from Bengali)

Let Thy worship, Thy hymns of praise
be the eternal solace of my life;

Let my life brim over with the songs
of Thy adoration, thoughts of Thy divine grace.

I shall see Thee, Mother, in the
wide open sky with wistful eyes.

I shall not ask for any boon,
say not a word; I shall only lay myself
down at Thy feet with tears of bliss.

I shall move about in Thy endless expanse of
heaven, scattering songs like flowers representing Thy glory.

I shall steep myself in Thy bliss, chanting Thy holy names
and sending their echoes throughout the Universe.

All my actions, all my thoughts of religion are Thy worship.
O Mother, give me *bhakti* (devotion), firm faith, so that
I may make Thy feet the sheet-anchor of my life.

Extract from the poem **Ma Anandamayi**
by Dilip Kumar Roy

From infancy we heard of mother Ind's
Long dynasties of sages high and hoary;
Yet in our Pantheons one seldom finds
A saintly woman's form haloed with glory.

We sing of the Gopies' Krishna-love sky-vast,
In the Vedas women wrote great hymns, we claim,
But when a woman harks back to the past,
We are vexed and never can find for it a name !

So Thou art born to us, O Damsel deep,
With wisdom and love divine, and with Thy sure
Answers and raptures make even stalwarts weep
And pandits laugh—one knows not with what lure !

O mystic Minstrel holding the Wizard's Wand !
O Envoy of the *Ethereal* to Clay !
Teach us until our minds can understand
Thy gospel of *Ānanda,* and come to stay !

In Remembrance

(A Jewish devotee from Germany)

Clothed in the glories of the Universe
around your head a crown of stars,
remote
and yet so near.
Bathing me in the still waves of peace and bliss.
With the essence
of all the beauties of the universe
soothing the sores of homesickness for Thy abode eternal
and feeding silently my heart.
Oh Ma !

—In remembrance, Solan 1946.

Ma !
Don't leave me in the turmoils
of this foolish world,
make me remember Thee, my real Self.
Then, in a twinkling of an eye
the clouding structures fall to pieces,
hiding no longer Thy shining Face.

—Europe 1967

Hymn composed by Bhāijī
(translated from Bengali)

Glory to Thee, Śrī Ānandamayī Mā, eternal holy dweller of the heart !

Thy lustre, Mother Nirmalā, illumines the universe. Heavenly virtues radiate from Thee, O Mother.

Queen of divine glory, Gouri,* *svāhā, svadhā,*† Om art Thou, O Mother.

Divinely graceful, Thou art absolute Reality, supremely beautiful and perfect, O Mother.

Sun and moon adorn Thy countenance, the boundless sky crowns Thy head,
the whole universe is Thy glorious form, O Mother.

The lustre of worldly riches art Thou, sweetness incarnate, radiant with splendour, O Mother.

Thou art charming as Lakṣmī is to Viṣṇu, Thou art peace, tranquillity and mercy; all gods and goddesses emanate from Thee, O Mother.

Grantor of happiness and benediction, bestower of love, wisdom and liberation art Thou, O Mother.

Bringing forth the world, Thou it is who nurses and preserves and finally draws it back into Thyself.

The very life of Thy devotees art Thou, Grace incarnate, Saviour of the three worlds, O Mother.

Spell of all Knowledge, charmer of yogins; the terrors of life are dispelled by Thy presence, O Mother.

The soul of all mantras art Thou, the revealer of the Vedas, pervading the whole universe, O Mother.

Thou art with forms and qualities, yet also formless and beyond all description; aglow with love and bliss, O Mother.

Thrilled by Thy touch, the entire universe, animate and inanimate, ever sings Thy praises, sweet Mother.

Let us all unite and from our hearts offer obeisance at Thy holy feet; hail, and again hail to Thee, Mother.

*Consort of Śiva.

†Svāhā and Svadhā interchangeably used, name of wife of Agni, the God of Fire. They preside over burnt offerings.

GLOSSARY

āsana yogic posture. Every posture corresponds to a particular state of mind.

āśrama hermitage. A place where seekers after Truth live together under the guidance of a Guru.

ātmā true Self. Supreme Existence or Being that is of the nature of Self-awareness and Self-delight, and behind all manifestations in nature.

avatāra descent of the Divine, usually in one of its aspects or powers. The object of such a descent is said to be the protection of moral order in the world.

bhāva spiritual ecstasy, generally emotional in nature.

brahmacāri religious student who devotes himself to spiritual practices and service and observes strict celibacy.

Brahman Supreme Reality conceived as one and undifferentiated, static as well as dynamic, yet above both.

brahmavidyā realization of immediate knowledge of the Brahman.

cakras psychic zones in the human system, which represent the fields of different psychic forces and which have to be conquered, purified and sublimated by the yogi on his upward journey to the sphere of divine consciousness and power.

dharma law of being. It signifies the inner principle of religion. Man's *dharma* is to realize his innate divinity. Also righteousness and duty.

darśana sight, vision. Having *darśana* of a deity or saint signifies to be blessed by his sight and presence.

gāyatrī sacred mantra of the Rigveda, a hymn to the sun, recited daily by Hindus of the three upper castes, after they have been invested with the sacred thread.

karma action, the result of action, as well as the law of cause and effect by which actions inevitably bear their fruit. Karma originates from the individual self in its ignorance functioning as an active agent. When man realizes his true Self, karma ceases for him.

kheyāla ordinarily a sudden psychic emergence, be it desire, will, attention, memory or knowledge. In Ānandamayī

Mā's case a spontaneous manifestation of divine Will.

kīrtana chanting or singing of the names or glories of God, performed by one person or a group of people.

līlā play. Movements and activities of the Supreme Being that are free by nature and not subject to laws. The cosmic show of duality is explained by the *vaiṣṇavas* as the *līlā* of God.

māyā the Supreme Divine Power by which the One conceals Itself and appears as the many.

ojhā exorcist of evil spirits.

prasāda food offered to a deity or saint becomes *prasāda* when it has been accepted and thereby blessed. It is then partaken of by the devotees.

pūjā ceremonial worship of the Hindus.

purdāh veil, screen; the seclusion of women.

ṛṣi seer. The *ṛṣis* are said to form a class of beings by themselves. Mantras are revealed to them.

sādhanā spiritual practice for the purpose of preparing oneself for Self-realization.

śākta worshipper of the divine Mother.

śakti divine Energy, usually symbolized by a woman.

samādhi state in which the mind is either completely concentrated on its object of contemplation, or ceases to function and only Pure Consciousness remains, revealing Itself to Itself.

saṁnyāsa renunciation. According to Hinduism the last stage of life, when family, possessions, caste, social position etc. are renounced and man surrenders himself to the Divine.

saṁnyāsī one who has taken the vow of renunciation.

satsaṅg literally fellowship with truth. The company of saints, sages and seekers after Truth. Religious meeting.

vaiṣṇava worshipper of Viṣṇu the Preserver and Sustainer of the universe or of one of His *avatāras*.

BIBLIOGRAPHICAL NOTE

The most important source for the life of Ānandamayī Mā is Brahmacārinī Gurupriyā Devi's *Srī Srī Mā Anandamayī* (3rd ed.; Bhadaini, Benares, 1956-76). So far seventeen volumes have appeared in Bengali and nineteen in Hindi. Shree Shree Anandamayee Sangha has published the following other works in Bengali: G. and B. Kirtti, *Ānandamayī Mā* (Bhadaini, Benares, 1952); Kumarcandra Bhattacarya (comp.), *Srī Srī Ānandamayī Upadeśamṛta-Saṃgraha* (Bhadaini, Benares, 1952); Gurupriyā Devi, *Akhaṇḍa Mahāyajña* (Bhadaini, Benares, n.d.); Bhaiji, *Mātṛdarśana* (3rd ed.; Bhadaini, Benares, 1966), translated into English by G. Das Gupta under the title *Mother as Revealed to Me* (4th ed.; Benares, 1972); Gurupriyā Devi, *Matṛvāṇi* (Bhadaini, Benares, n.d.), translated into English by Brahmacārini Ātmānanda under the title *Matri Vani* (4th ed. 1977). Shree Shree Anandamayee Sangha also published in English *Mother as Seen by Her Devotees* (3rd ed.; Bhadaini, Benares, 1976) and *Words of Sri Anandamayi Ma*, trans. and comp. by Ātmānanda (Benares, 1961). B. Mukerji, *From the Life of Sri Anandamayi Ma* (Bhadaini, Benares, 1970). *Mā Ānandamayī Līlā*, Memoirs of Hari Ram Joshi (Varanasi 1974). Shyamananda Banerjee: *A Mystic Sage Ma Anandamayi* (Calcutta 1973.) The quarterly, *Ānanda Vārtā*, has been published since 1952 in Bengali, Hindi, and English. There is a German work: Melita Maschmann, *Der Tiger singt Kirtana* (Weilheim, Oberbayern: Otto Wilhelm Barth-Verlag, 1967) and a French work: Armaud Desjardins, *Ashrams-Les yogis at les sages* (Paris: La Palatine, n.d.). Translations of Ma Anandamayi's teaching in French: *Mātri Vāni* (Panharmonie, 70 Bd M. Barres, Neuilly-sur-Seine) and *L'Enseignement de Mā Anandamayi*, Traduit par Josette Herbert. Preface de Jean et Josette Herbert. (Editions Albin Michel, Paris 1974).

Some information concerning Ānandamayī Mā can also be found in Paramahansa Yogananda, *Autobiography of a Yogi* (New York: Philosophical Library, 1946) and in Alexander Lipski, "Some Aspects of the Life and Teachings of the East Bengal Saint Ānandamayī Mā," *History of Religions* IX, no. 1 (August, 1969), 59-77.